BREXIT BORIS

FROM MAYOR TO NIGHTMARE

HEATHCOTE WILLIAMS

publicreading
ROOMS
www.prruk.org

Published in 2016 by Public Reading Rooms
Visit our website at www.prruk.org

ISBN 978-0-9955352-0-6

HEATHCOTE WILLIAMS
Publications include *Whale Nation, Royal Babylon, Sacred Elephant, Forbidden Fruit, Autogeddon* and *Badshah Khan - Islamic Peace Warrior*. As an actor he has appeared in many films, including *The Tempest, Wish You Were Here, Orlando*, and *Alice in Wonderland*.

FEATURED CARTOONISTS
Steve Bell, Peter Brookes, Dave Brown, Andy Davey, Martin Rowson, Gerald Scarfe, Ralph Steadman

The front cover image is by ©Peter Brookes

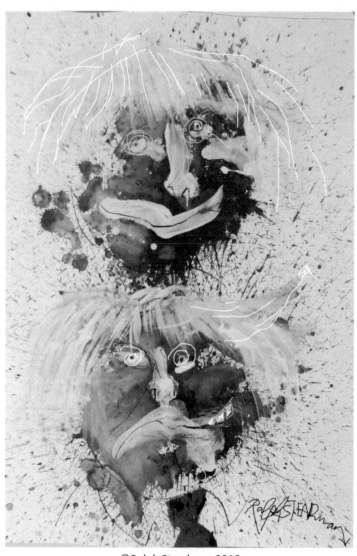

©Ralph Steadman 2016

Just because you are a character doesn't mean you have character. **- The Wolf in *Pulp Fiction***

BREXIT BORIS

FROM MAYOR TO NIGHTMARE

Contents

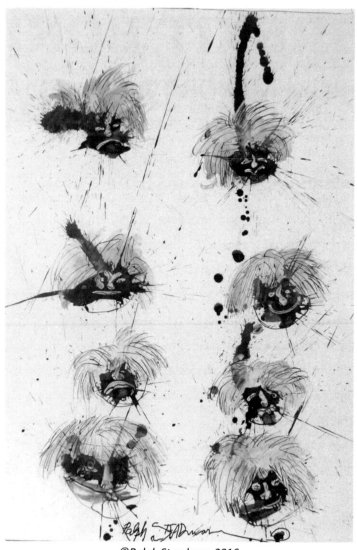

©Ralph Steadman 2016

1

Bubbles of Dissent and Suspicion

©Andy Davey 2016

SOME TEN THOUSAND YEARS ago Britain was physically attached to the European landmass, and twelve hundred years ago a pan-European identity was established amongst Europe's inhabitants by Charlemagne. It had its own euro currency on a silver standard, namely the mark. It's been said of Charlemagne that, as if by a flick of a switch, he turned on the light that ended the Dark Ages.

Europe's pre-history makes the protestations of the 'little Englanders', as George Orwell would doubtless have called the anxious xenophobes who've been wishing to withdraw from the European experiment, seem ludicrous.

Despite the calculations of the various number crunchers of the 'Leave Europe Now' and 'Brexit' brigades in Britain, they are surely irrelevant to the overriding importance of there being another, and a qualitatively different, power bloc in the world—a power bloc which, in the words of the preamble to the 2005 European Constitution, is intended to draw inspiration "from the cultural, religious and humanist inheritance of Europe, from which have developed the universal values of the inviolable and inalienable rights of the human person, freedom, democracy, equality and the rule of law".

Severe criticism can be levelled at the European Union, particularly against its austerity and its cuts agenda. It is undemocratic and remote from the lived experience of its peoples. Despite its many failings, however, European courts have nonetheless enforced important environmental legislation that might never have seen the light of day if the issues had been left to individual and sovereign parliaments.

European courts have also upheld a spirit of fair play and equal rights in relation to the needs of Europe's labour forces. They've capped bankers' bonuses, and Europe has a unique Convention on Human Rights which acknowledges man's freedom of movement. (Europe has, after all, only come into existence thanks to invasions of hunter-gatherers from Africa.)

Most importantly perhaps the European Union has had, post-World War II, an historic and a constitutional desire to prevent and resolve conflict—conflicts having ravaged Europe with increasing devastation for a thousand years.

However, in certain parts of Europe there are bubbles of resistance—feverish bubbles of nationalistic dissent and exaggerated suspicion which threaten the European ideal, as symbolised in its anthem taken from Beethoven's *Ode to Joy*, an anthem that includes such lines as: "Unity is our future - Long live Europe, come what may!" and "North and South will work together / Just as friends and neighbours should. East and West will grow together - Brotherhood and Sisterhood!"

In its desire to absent itself from such improving, albeit naive, sentiments, Britain has lately become infected by a self-regarding miasma, made manifest by the appearance of the UK Independence Party—a kind of Waitrose[1] version of the BNP[2]—together with a retrospective and scowling rump within the Tory Party, both of which hark back to another, ungenerous age where there was no need to take cognizance of 'Johnny Foreigner'.

©Ralph Steadman 2016

2

Enter 'National Treasure' Boris Johnson

©Peter Brookes 2016 (after John Hassall)

BORIS JOHNSON has been the most vocal of those lining up to wrench the country they claim to love away from the dastardly clutches of a Europe which they see as undermining their sovereignty and hence their own power. They do not want to love their neighbour. They want to divorce him.

Johnson is someone whom the right-wing media are fond of describing as a 'national treasure'. He has a bumbling, blustering manner which some find engaging and others tiresome. He'll unfailingly ruffle his hair before a TV appearance in order to give the calculated impression of harmless eccentricity. He specialises in self-deprecation which some find winning and others calculated.

Johnson has admitted that he employs self-deprecation as a manipulative ploy, to disarm his potential enemies. In an interview with the American TV channel CNBC he declared:

"Self-deprecation is a very cunning device ... all about understanding that basically people regard politicians as a bunch of shysters, so you've got to be understood ... that's what it's all about, I suppose."[3]

In the light of what lies behind his muddled façade, namely a ruthless and often cruel ambition together with an elitism and a ferocious temper when challenged, it is wrong-headed to describe such a man as a 'national treasure'. Johnson is a man who values himself and his own agenda much more highly than he does the nation or the nation's interest.

His friends say of him approvingly, as if it was a virtue, "Boris is about Boris". They're saying this, of course, because they admire the man's remorseless self-promotion and perhaps because, as enthusiastic members of the cult of Boris, they look forward to bathing in his stardust should he become Prime Minister. For that's what he has most assuredly set his heart on, and what in his madder moments he has spoken of as his "destiny" if not his birthright.[4] The European issue has been the trampoline upon which Boris Johnson thought he could bounce his 17-stone self into Number 10 Downing Street.

'Beano Boris', or 'Bonking Boris' as the satirical magazine *Private Eye* (always at a loss as to why anyone should take Johnson seriously) calls him, has made his pitch for the top job his life's work.

The prospect has not been universally well received. In a guest column for the *New Statesman*, Boris's former colleague on the *Daily* and *Sunday Telegraph*, Simon Heffer, claims that "Even Boris's senior colleagues dread Tory activists handing him the keys to Downing Street".

Heffer points out that "it is little wonder that the campaign to leave the European Union was so thrilled to receive Johnson's belated—and confused—endorsement last month.

"However, he did what the campaign views as the right thing for the wrong reason. When Johnson worked with me in the mid-

1990s an Oxford contemporary warned me about him, saying he was the most rampantly ambitious person he had ever met and that he believed in nothing apart from himself."

Heffer begins his column by saying, damningly: "Some people feel that Boris Johnson can do no wrong. They are often those who live vicariously through the celebrities seen on television and followed on the internet, and for whom entertainment is an important distraction. Most entertainment is harmless—no wars have been started or economies wrecked by *I'm a Celebrity - Get Me Out of Here!* or *Strictly Come Dancing*. However, our education in citizenship should extend to understanding that when a politician becomes entertainment first and foremost there is a danger that he, or she, may lack the requisites of statesmanship."[5]

Shortly after his announcement in February 2016 that he was backing the Brexit campaign to leave Europe, Johnson's long-smouldering antipathy to Prime Minister Cameron was made public in the House of Commons. When Cameron was explaining in detail what it was that he'd negotiated in Europe on behalf of his country, Boris could be heard several times boorishly shouting "Rubbish!" in quick and emphatic succession, then looking around him in the hope that his fellow MPs would join him in the ribald barracking of his leader.

Johnson has something about him that feels at home in a braying mob. In his campaign to restore foxhunting (now illegal) and in his preposterous urging of his fellow-Londoners to take up foxhunting as a way of dealing with urban foxes (Johnson was distressed when the family cat was snapped at by a visiting fox) he is clearly unafraid of the implications of Oscar Wilde's description of foxhunting as the "pursuit of the uneatable by the unspeakable". There are many ways in which Johnson qualifies as unspeakable.

The following quotes should be enough to convey a sense of the mind-set of this 'national treasure' whom the governing party in Britain has been turning into a cult figure and crediting with inflated gifts such as his being able to rebrand the Tory Party, so often nicknamed "the nasty party".

Unfortunately for such a project, Johnson has more than his own share of nastiness. He talks of migrants who "leech, bludge and scrounge"[6] off taxpayers. Visiting Uganda, Johnson cheerily said to UN workers and their black driver: "Right, let's go and look at some more piccaninnies"[7]—a racist word notoriously used by the Tory MP Enoch Powell in his 'rivers of blood' speech against immigration.

Johnson likens Chinese workers to "puffing coolies"[8] and he even favours a return to colonial rule for Africa: "Left to their own devices," Johnson has proclaimed, "the natives would rely on nothing but the instant carbohydrate gratification of the plantain."[9]

More egregiously still, he adds: "The problem is not that we were once in charge, but that we are not in charge any more."[10] He accused Nelson Mandela of moving Africa towards a "tyranny of black majority rule".[11] And he also used his column in the *Spectator* to claim that the Stephen Lawrence inquiry was a "witch-hunt" against the police.[12]

On his watch as editor of the *Spectator* from 1999 to 2005, Johnson happily published the Greek playboy 'Taki' with his idle fulminations on "Bongo-bongo land", [13] on West Indians "multiplying like flies"[14] (which prompted a police probe) and on "black hoodlums" being the root of Britain's social ills. When talking of a "world Jewish conspiracy" the Neanderthal Taki describes himself as a "*soi-disant* anti-semite".[15] Other Taki columns that appeared, with editor Johnson's implied blessing, defended the Greek fascist organization, Golden Dawn ("A fascist takeover of Greece? We should be so lucky"),[16] claimed that ethnic minorities had lower IQs and stated that black NBA basketball players walk around with their arms hanging down and their tongues sticking out.[17]

Rather than fire Taki for his arrant racism or even take him to task, Johnson threw a party for him in October 2000 to celebrate Taki's "25 glorious years" as a *Spectator* columnist.

Johnson's sexism doesn't lag far behind: "The chicks in the *GQ* expenses department—and if you can't call them chicks, then what the hell, I ask you, is the point of writing for *GQ*." For the benefit of readers of the *Spectator* Johnson claims to have invented the Tottometer—"the Geiger-counter that detects good-looking women".[18] Appointing him as editor was, in the words of one *Spectator* contributor, like "entrusting a Ming vase to an ape".[19]

Johnson derided renewable energy and opposed the Kyoto Treaty on climate change.[20] He supported the homophobic Section 28 legislation and once compared civil partnerships to the marriage of "three men and a dog".[21] As mayor of London, he scrapped the pledge of the previous mayor, Ken Livingstone, to make 50 per cent of all new homes cheap enough for ordinary London workers—a move likely to mean the collapse of buying and renting markets, and which will do little to correct excesses that have seen single properties changing hands for £200 million. Some areas of London are now in pitch darkness because they're being kept vacant by absentee speculators—parasitic profiteers who invest in property rather than inhabit it. "As homelessness grows," says Denis MacShane, "Europe needs a policy of housing which stops homes being bought as a chip in the casino of modern frontier-free markets but never lived in."[22]

While the ranks of the homeless in London are burgeoning, the super-rich are driving up property prices by seeking out a guaranteed return on their wealth, and they have had Boris Johnson to support them. "We should be humbly thanking the super-rich, not bashing them", he says. "They are victims just like the homeless."

These are the "zillionaires", Johnson writes, "who have other people almost everywhere to do their bidding: people to drive their cars and people to pick up their socks and people to rub their temples with eau de cologne and people to bid for the Munch etching at Christie's".

Johnson is impressed by gargantuan wealth and feels that any resentment of it is misplaced, since in Johnson's view super-rich zillionaires should be offered our "hearty thanks". The top one per cent of earners pay 29.8 per cent of all income tax and, according to Johnson, put "bread on the tables of families who—if the rich didn't invest in supercars and employ eau de cologne-dabbers—might otherwise find themselves without a breadwinner".

Contrastingly, US presidential candidate, Bernie Sanders says: "There is something profoundly wrong when the top one-tenth of 1 per cent owns almost as much wealth as the bottom 90 per cent, and when 99 per cent of all new income goes to the top 1 per cent"

But if Boris Johnson believes in anything, then he clearly believes in a greed-driven and elitist economy—he's a plutocrat praising bankers whose main product is debt.

The idea that each day, capitalism kills far more innocents than died on 9/11, as Dennis Rahkonen has shown, does not register on the radar of Planet Boris.[23] It's alien to his thought processes. It's irrelevant.

The implications of some of Johnson's other views are equally life-threatening: he has opposed the smoking ban despite improvements in health and atmosphere in pubs.

Furthermore, in much the same way as Ronald Reagan alleged that "Trees cause more pollution than automobiles do",[24] Johnson has perversely called pedestrians "the most dangerous features on the roads".[25] In his time as mayor, he vowed to speed up traffic by letting motorbikes use bus lanes, and he adjusted traffic signal timings to give priority to vehicles and less time for pedestrians to cross the road.

Green Party member of the London Assembly Darren Johnson commented: "A broad look back at the outgoing mayor's record on road safety shows that the overall number of casualties of all severities has gone up by 5 per cent under Boris Johnson. This is in contrast to the previous mayor Ken Livingstone, who reduced the toll by 38 per cent in eight years. In real numbers that means over 2,500 more people were injured last year than in 2008, the year Boris Johnson became mayor."[26]

As a motorist who reviews cars for *GQ*, the men's magazine, Johnson presents himself, in the words of his biographer, Sonia Purnell, as "a sex-obsessed cross between Jeremy Clarkson and Toad of Toad Hall".

"There is talk", she notes, "of blonde drivers 'waggling their rumps', his own superior horsepower 'taking them from behind', aided by tantalising thoughts of the imaginary 'ample bosoms' of the female Sat Nav voice."[27]

Purnell exposes Johnson's desperate desire to display his "virile superiority" as he describes a Nissan Murano as "a sort of fat-lipped SUV on steroids" and she quotes from his revealing review: "Tee-hee!" Johnson coos. "What was it saying, with the plutocratic sneer of that gleaming grille? It was saying 'out of my way, small car driven by ordinary person on modest income. Make way for Murano!'"[28]

More seriously cringe-making was Johnson's support for the Iraq War in 2003 and the crass nature of his support. He was to write in the *Daily Telegraph*: "That is the best case for Bush; that, among other things, he liberated Iraq. It is good enough for me."[29] He would say enthusiastically of the absurd but deadly US president: "Whenever he appears on TV, I find a cheer rising irresistibly in my throat."[30]

Yet there is scant consistency in his views. Johnson would make it clear when he was editing the *Spectator*, the influential conservative weekly, that he was giving Bush his full support.

"Not only did I want Bush to win", Johnson claimed, revealing a lamentable absence of political judgment, "but we threw the entire weight of the *Spectator* behind him."[31]

Perversely, in the same year as Johnson claims to be supporting Bush so effusively, he writes in a *Spectator* leader entitled 'Infantile resentment': "The President is a cross-eyed Texan warmonger, unelected, inarticulate, who epitomises the arrogance of American foreign policy."[32]

This and his other vagaries represent something of a political bi-polarity. Johnson's time-serving mind-set enables him to pretend, for example, that he's never uttered a negative word about Nelson Mandela, although Johnson's generation of young Tories would frequently recommend that Mandela be hanged.

Johnson himself would sneeringly refer to Mandela as "the sainted one" and rue the day that the white apartheid regime had been replaced by majority black rule.[33] He expressed contempt for celebrities such as Imran Khan and Naomi Campbell, who he said liked to bathe in Mandela's reflected glory. They had, in his view, "left reason behind".[34]

On being asked for a quote upon Mandela's death, Johnson declares: "I never in my life deviated from the position of fervent, fervent admiration for Nelson Mandela."

When one minute Johnson is cracking homophobic jokes about "tank-topped bum-boys", and the next he is urging the gay community to support him in voting for Brexit on the grounds of the prevalence of gay oppression in Eastern Europe, it is no wonder that Conrad Black, then the *Spectator*'s owner, characterised Johnson as "ineffably duplicitous".

Worse however than Boris provoking the ire of the soon-to-be discredited jailbird Black, was how he routinely aroused the suspicion and irritation of his fellow journalists. Rory Watson, a Press Association correspondent who worked in Brussels at the same time as Johnson, has claimed that Johnson "made up stories". David Usborne of *The Independent* considers Johnson to be "fundamentally intellectually dishonest in my view. He was serving his masters in a very skilful way but I never felt he believed a word."[35] And Johnson's Etonian contemporary James Landale, now a senior BBC political editor, went into verse about the lies of Boris the journalist—having experienced them at first hand in Brussels:

Boris told such dreadful lies
It made one gasp and stretch one's eyes.

3

Boris Titillates the Europhobes

©Martin Rowson 2016

IN 1989 BORIS JOHNSON arrived in Brussels to work for the *Daily Telegraph*, having just been fired by the *Times* for inventing quotations and attributing them to an Oxford professor at Balliol College, Dr Colin Lucas, who—since Lucas was Boris Johnson's own godfather—had no reason to mistrust him. Lucas' trust proved misplaced.

Dr Lucas was an archaeologist who had discovered the remains of Edward II's 14th century 'Rosary' Palace in Hay's Wharf on the south bank of the Thames. To spice up a story for his employer, Johnson saw fit to fabricate a comment from his godfather about the monarch's sexual exploits with his favourite, Piers Gaveston. Johnson falsely quoted Professor Lucas as saying the King "had enjoyed a reign of dissolution with his catamite, Piers Gaveston" in the palace.

Unfortunately for Johnson, the palace was built in 1325 and Gaveston had been beheaded in 1312. Johnson had at no point bothered to discuss the subject in any relevant detail with his godfather.

Fearful of the damage to his academic reputation, an angry, betrayed and humiliated Lucas got in touch with the *Times* and complained. According to Andrew Gilmour, who was at Balliol with both Lucas and Johnson, "Lucas was a laughing stock. Every sub-lecturer from Sheffield wrote in to point out his error."[36]

When quizzed by the *Times'* editor, Charlie Wilson, Johnson made the mistake of digging the hole he was in more deeply. He insisted that he'd spoken to Lucas and that he'd got the erroneous information from him. But of course he hadn't. He was lying. Misled by Johnson, the editor of the *Times* wrote to Lucas saying: "Our reporter stands by his story." The hurt and angry Lucas complained again.

The *Times* now took Johnson's breach of their journalistic code seriously: for attributing his own historical mistake to that of a distinguished archaeologist and historian, for sexing up the story at Lucas' expense, and for lying to the *Times* about having spoken to Lucas to obtain the quote when he hadn't done so at all. Johnson was fired.

The parliamentary sketch-writer, Simon Hoggart, wittily commented that it was all "amazing, since it means that yesterday Piers Gaveston had brought a national leader to his knees for the first time in 700 years".[37]

Challenged about this later, Johnson attempted to play it down[38] by saying that he'd just "mildly sandpapered something someone said". Even now he continues to blame "fact-grubbing historians" for his *Times* downfall.[39]

Given such a past, it might be thought that on arriving in

Brussels to work for the *Daily Telegraph*, Johnson would pay more attention to the truth, but the reverse proved to be the case.

The first story Johnson filed concerned the Berlaymont building in Brussels, the headquarters of the European Commission. During the building's refurbishment it had to be evacuated due to an asbestos problem. In Johnson's hands, however, the story is re-jigged in order to titillate the Europhobia of the *Daily Telegraph*'s owners and readers. The building, a symbol of European governance, was, Johnson claimed, to be "blown up". But it wasn't. The news story that Johnson had filed was quite untrue—a wishful fantasy to curry favour with his employers.

Shortly afterwards he followed this up with another story, this time for the *Sunday Telegraph*: "Delors Plan to Rule Europe." Again this was perhaps more influenced by some projection of Johnson's own mythomaniac childhood—his toddler ambition to be "the World King" and later to be president of the United States[40] (he was born in New York and until recently held a US passport)—rather than by any salient facts.

Johnson wrote that it had been "reported that Delors wanted to scrap the rotation of the EU presidency and to centralize power in Brussels. The member states would lose their remaining veto rights."[41]

But it wasn't true. It was an invention. However there was a sub-text: the popular British tabloids had begun to specialise in shock-horror stories about the EU, deliberately designed to create fears about Europe and invariably untrue. In September 1994, for example, all of the British tabloids insisted that Brussels was going to ban curved or small bananas. Only straight bananas were to be sold. This was untrue.

On 21 February 2005, the *Sun* claimed that "EU health chiefs are drawing up plans to close thousands of British off-licences". This was false.

Here is the *Daily Star* on the same date: "Supermarkets will only be able to sell booze at weekends under secret plans by barmy Brussels bureaucrats." This was untrue.

Not to be outdone, in October 1997, the *Daily Mail* claimed that the EU was "about to abolish the British loaf. Brussels bureaucrats are planning the end of the British standard loaf." Untrue, as a visit to any British supermarket would reveal.

In his book on Brexit, the former Labour MP, Denis Mac-Shane, suggested: "It would take a whole book to list all the myths and half-truths about Europe."

Interestingly, MacShane goes on "to trace a starting point" and he singles out Boris Johnson as being the man who "invented Eurosceptic news reporting". According to MacShane, "The arrival of Boris Johnson as the Brussels correspondent of the *Daily Telegraph* in 1989, a year after Mrs Thatcher's Bruges speech[42], was the moment when telling lies about Europe became official British newspaper policy. The *Daily Telegraph* was also in foreign ownership and was on the eve of becoming the cheerleader for crude anti-European ideology."[43]

Here is an example of such crudity, in a typical Johnson canard: "First they make us pay in our taxes for Greek olive groves, many of which probably don't exist. Then they say we can't dip our bread in olive oil in restaurants. We didn't join the Common Market—betraying the New Zealanders and their butter—in order to be told when, where and how we must eat the olive oil we have been forced to subsidize."[44] Another fabrication, of course.

The trend pioneered by Johnson continued relentlessly up to the 2016 Referendum, as in the *Daily Express* headline proclaiming: "Europe steals our coastline"[45], when in truth, instead of there being any vampire-like Europe responsible for the coastal erosion of neighbouring British islands, the story would turn out merely to be concerned with the EU trying to coordinate coastguards in order to improve their response to refugees at sea.

On the eve of the referendum, one of Johnson's colleagues in Brussels, the former *Times* correspondent Martin Fletcher, chose his Facebook page to spill the beans:

For 25 years our press has fed the British public a diet of distorted, mendacious and relentlessly hostile stories about the EU—and the journalist who set the tone was Boris Johnson ... He seized every chance to mock or denigrate the EU, filing stories that were undoubtedly colourful but also grotesquely exaggerated or completely untrue. The Telegraph loved it. So did the Tory Right. Johnson's reports also had an amazing, explosive effect on the rest of Fleet Street ... By the time I arrived in Brussels editors only wanted stories about faceless Brussels' Eurocrats imposing absurd rules on Britain, or scheming Europeans ganging up on us, or British prime ministers fighting plucky rearguard actions against a hostile continent. Much of Fleet Street seemed unable to view the EU through any other prism. It was the only narrative it was interested in ... Boris Johnson is now campaigning against the cartoon caricature of the EU that he himself created. He is campaigning against a largely fictional EU that bears no relation to reality.

One of the most frequent charges made against the EU by Johnson and his secessionists, the 'little Englanders', is that it is undemocratic. However they persistently overlook the fact that they each have an MEP, a Member of the European Parliament whom they can vote in and out.

In their arguments against Britain remaining in the Union they like to refer, with a self-satisfied patriotism, to their own Parliament as being the living exemplar of democracy, the mother of parliaments no less; and hence, they say, it would be quite wrong for them to devolve one iota of that Parliament's sovereignty to the undemocratic and demonised Brussels.

By a comic irony, however, a closer look at the British Parliament reveals a highly undemocratic institution housed within the Palace of Westminster.

To begin with, its proceedings can only be set in motion when they have been inaugurated or 'opened' by a monarch who owes her undemocratic position to heredity and who is, by contrast with most of her subjects, one of the richest women in the world.

Then, as if in some enormous and neo-feudal stately home, some five thousand servants work within the building, where they bow and scrape in its heavily subsidised restaurants and bars and offices to a group of state officials in both the House of Commons and the House of Lords—the largest proportion of the latter being entirely unelected.

There is, in fact—as revealed by simple arithmetic—a preponderance of legislators within Parliament who have absolutely no democratic mandate whatsoever. There are, for example, twenty-six bishops, representatives of the state religion, the Church of England, and the House of Lords is stacked to its undemocratic rafters with wealthy party donors—pleased to have discovered that a million pounds or two will secure them a peerage.

Honours have been for sale since the baronetcy, a quaint hereditary knighthood, was devised by King James in the early 17th century specifically to raise cash—subtly so, but unquestionably for sale. When Lord Salisbury became prime minister for the first time in 1885, he said that dealing with those who aspired to become lords or knights had "been a revelation to me of the baser side of human nature". Which was echoed by Lord Curzon: "People are rather apt, supposing they see in the newspapers that an honour has been conferred upon some person unknown to themselves, to imagine that the honour has been bought." People's enduring ability to sense mephitic stenches hovering around the honours system is well-placed. The chain-store grocer, David Sainsbury, gives two million to the Labour Party on long loan and then, *mirabile dictu*, he becomes Lord Sainsbury. There are continuing examples too numerous to mention.

With its 792 members, the House of Lords overflows with tuft-hunters—its dubiously ennobled and favoured appointees—and it is the only second chamber in the world which is larger than its Parliament's first chamber: the elected House of Commons has just 650 members.

The mother of parliaments is thus intrinsically undemocratic and it even invites comparison with Iran, which is the only other state legislature that includes representatives of the state religion as of right.

Here is Boris Johnson on the allegations of gravy-train politics in the EU: "With every year of its existence, the Euro-parliament deepens the general suspicion of the public—that the EU is a racket, and that the MEPs are on a gigantic boondoggle."[46]

At the same time Johnson wrote this, however, he was earning £250,000 per year from writing Europhobic articles for the *Daily Telegraph* (a hefty sum he grandiosely dismissed as 'chicken feed' on the BBC programme *Hardtalk* and which would later rise to £500,000). For several years Johnson would also be combining this with his mayoral salary of £150,000.

Since his own snout was so very firmly in the trough he could hardly make allegations about EU gravy-train politics and he was most certainly in no position to do so when his own employment policy at the Eurosceptic *Spectator* would reek of nepotistic corruption.

So keen was Johnson on allowing the *Spectator* to serve his own ends that at one point it came to be nicknamed the *Johnsonator*. Johnson used it, for example, to give frequent employment to his brother Leo, to his sister Rachel, and to her husband Ivo Dawnay. His father Stanley was hired to write on the environment, and his father-in-law Charles Wheeler was engaged to write on foreign affairs.[47]

The Johnson dynasty's lust for self-promotion is notorious. The paterfamilias of the Johnson brood, Stanley Johnson, "never ceases to trumpet their achievements, even ostentatiously counting the number of times his family appears in one day's newspapers in the public arena of his local newsagent".[48]

4

From Mayor to Nightmare

©Peter Brookes 2016

IN 2008 BORIS JOHNSON was elected Mayor of London. In his first year in office, he personally spent £4,698 on taxis. One journey alone cost the taxpayer £237, prompting a witty blogger to comment: "Where exactly does Boris cycle. Is it just to and from photo-shoots?"[49]

Johnson riding a bicycle around town can, of course, have as much to do with his projecting Brand Boris as it does with any serious environmental concerns. He keeps two cars after all in his £2.3 million Georgian townhouse overlooking the Regent's Canal. Boris may be an intermittent climate change denier, but a bicycle can enable him to feel superior.

On one occasion Johnson made a great show of pitting his bicycle against what he thought was a ministerial car in which the Labour MP Keith Vaz was travelling. According to Johnson, as the vehicle passed him on a street in Whitehall, "Vaz hauled down the window to hail me. Actually, I can't be sure that it was Vaz who pressed the button. It might have been him, or the driver, or the bodyguard."

Keith Vaz then graciously offered Johnson a lift. However, in an article in the *Daily Telegraph*, entitled 'Limo-Loving Politicians', Johnson would describe the lift as having been offered "in the kindly tones of Louis XIV leaning from his carriage to comfort a poor peasant woman struggling along in the mud". Johnson refuses. "'No, it's OK, thanks, Keith', I said, slapping the battered old handlebars of my machine, 'I've got my bike.'"

Johnson then decried the cost to the taxpayer of Vaz's "grandiose entourage". Here was Vaz, Johnson added, "cruising around London as though he was Charles bloody de Gaulle". For good measure he castigated Vaz's "rear end" as the "symbol of everything wrong with British politics"—it being, Johnson claimed, "cupped, cosseted, cocooned on the velour upholstery of a government car".

The only problem with Johnson's story was that Vaz's behind was in fact firmly planted on the seat of the Vaz family's Prius. For, as a mere select committee chairman, Vaz was not entitled to a ministerial car let alone to have a chauffeur or a bodyguard and on this occasion the car was in fact being driven by Vaz's assistant and so Johnson's sneering fantasy was, in Vaz's words, "all a nonsense".[50]

Johnson had twisted a non-event to his own ends and had maliciously tried to put Keith Vaz in a bad light simply in order to earn his quarter to half a million pound salary from the *Daily Telegraph*.[51]

Johnson's distortion of the facts to suit himself was evident at Oxford if not before. When he was an undergraduate, Johnson had fervently wished to become president of the Oxford Union, widely considered a stepping-stone to political success in the outside world. It was a post for which the Oxford Union rulebook forbade outright canvassing. However, cavalierly ignoring Union procedure, Johnson set about canvassing vigorously on his own behalf: "On one occasion he even handed out bottles of red wine to Gridiron members in a particularly brazen, even crass attempt to 'buy' their votes. Such displays of naked ambition were totally out of place, recalls one undergraduate there that day."[52]

On another occasion, Johnson tried to bamboozle his way into the presidential office by deception. Judging the Conservative Party to be less popular amongst Oxford's student body than in the shires he told Union members—his potential voters—that he was a member of the SDP, the Social Democratic Party. He was not.

To his chagrin he was not elected. His state-school rival Neil Sherlock, who had a rather broader appeal, was returned with a sizeable majority despite Johnson having got his glamorous girlfriend, Allegra Mostyn-Owen, to try and persuade Sherlock behind the scenes "not to stand against 'my Boris'".[53]

Sonia Purnell describes how "a good deal of snobbish and unpleasant personal abuse was heaped on Sherlock by Boris supporters who pulled faces and called him a 'horrible, spermy little man', who spoke with a 'funny accent' and who was 'patently uncharismatic'".[54]

In the run-up to his election as London Mayor, Johnson would adopt a similar ploy for his campaign hustings to that which he employed at the Oxford Union. At a meeting of the London Citizens' Convention in Westminster's Methodist Central Hall, Johnson described himself as "the grandson of a Muslim immigrant from Turkey". He fondly hoped this would counteract all the 'racist' chatter about him, but since his self-description was inaccurate, it didn't.[55]

On Johnson's second try at being elected to the Oxford Union he was successful and he would explain this subsequent success in an essay called 'Politics'. What you needed, according to Johnson, was "a disciplined and deluded collection of stooges" to get the vote out for you in their respective colleges.

Andrew Gimson, Johnson's first biographer, says this analysis of how to become president of the Oxford Union was "worthy of Machiavelli".[56]:

> *The key word here is 'deluded'. Johnson's stooges were recruited by his trick of intimating that he'd do something for them once elected even if he had every intention of forgetting all about them. Johnson reveals his cynically manipulative technique: "The relationship ... is founded on duplicity". Johnson goes on: "The tragedy of the stooge is that even if he thinks this through, he wants so much to believe that his relationship with the candidate is special that he shuts out the truth. The terrible art of the candidate is to coddle the self-deception of the stooge."[57]*

Such behaviour didn't make him popular. Lloyd Evans, the editor of the Oxford University satirical magazine, *Tributary*, noted that during the build-up to the Union Presidency election, "he [Johnson] became fixated about what we were writing about him".

They were preparing an issue which "contained a whole stream of abuse of Boris. We called him an exiled Armenian chicken farmer. The other thing we called him was the Aryan bull pig, victim of a hideous Nazi war experiment in 1936. We'd also call him incompetent. That was the thing he picked up on [...] He was absolutely incandescent. He really went mad. He grabbed the typewriter and said, 'Damn it I'm a journalist', and started writing his own version of the whole thing. We ended up not publishing any of it. I was surprised by how angry he was."[58] Elsewhere Evans is quoted as saying that Johnson's anger "was coming from a deep, dark place".[59]

Ever unpredictable, opportunistic and volatile, Johnson rivals

Donald Trump, to whom he bears a certain similarity. Johnson has been described as "Trump with a thesaurus" and he shares with Trump a shameless ability to contradict himself and yet to believe that he's right on each occasion. They also share the notion that they have a licence to lie—particularly if they can come up with a vivid enough excuse to mask their deception.

The master-in-college at Eton, Martin Hammond, would say of Johnson: "Boris sometimes seems affronted when criticised [...] I think he honestly believes that it is churlish of us not to regard him as an exception."[60]

Famously, Johnson would characterise reports he had cheated on his wife with a colleague at the *Spectator*, Petronella Wyatt, as "an inverted pyramid of piffle". This oddly phrased denial was to no avail, however, when the affair was confirmed by Petronella Wyatt's mother, and when various friends of Wyatt inconveniently briefed newspapers that she'd had two abortions and that she'd understandably felt betrayed by the then Tory arts spokesman.[61]

Johnson's instinctive dishonesty was clear from their relationship. "Faced with one of Petronella's pregnancies, he said she should have an affair with someone and say it was their child."[62]

His dishonesty colours another relationship with one Helen Macintyre whom Johnson appointed as his arts adviser when he was mayor. Johnson, dubbed "our Berlusconi" by Ian Hislop, has had a child with Macintyre but, despite the glaring evidence of the child's albino-cum-blond hair of its father, Johnson insists that the child's hair is "ginger".[63] It isn't.

In 2013, the Court of Appeal dismissed an attempt by a former mistress to stop publication of information about her child with Johnson, ruling that his "recklessness" was "a public interest matter which the electorate was entitled to know when considering his fitness for high public office".

The judge might also have ruled that his dishonesty too could be construed as a matter of public concern. It was certainly thought to be of concern to his former editor on the *Daily Telegraph*, the military historian Max Hastings:

"Boris is a gold medal egomaniac. I would not trust him with my wife nor—from painful experience—with my wallet. It is unnecessary to take any moral view about his almost crazed infidelities, but it is hard to believe that any man so conspicuously incapable of controlling his own libido is fit to be trusted with controlling the country. He is also a far more ruthless, and frankly nastier figure than the public appreciates."[64]

Unfortunately for Johnson, his dishonesty proved too much for Michael Howard, his then Party leader. Howard was to sack him from his junior Cabinet post for lying about the Wyatt affair.

While Boris Johnson's fans like to describe him as "political Viagra", he can be described less attractively but with equal accuracy as a louche and incompetent bully to whom lying comes as second nature and who has a distinctly unpleasant fascination with violence.

In a *Vanity Fair* profile, the writer Michael Wolff tailed Johnson for a day or two and listened to his speeches. Wolff commented: "It's all riff—anti-political correctness, anti-personal regulation, pro the verities of English life (hunting and smoking and smacking)."[65]

Depending on your point of view, Boris Johnson's beloved English 'verities' can equally be described as animal torture, self-harm and child abuse.

He is pro-hunting and in promoting the cause he reveals how he has benefited gastronomically from stag hunting on Exmoor where his father, Stanley Johnson, owns some five hundred acres. The stag in question was surrounded by the hounds in the middle of the river Exe: "I can see it now," Johnson recalls, "stepping high in the water, eyes rolling, tongue protruding, foaming, antlers streaming bracken and leaves like the hat of some demented old woman, and behind is the sexual, high-pitched yipping of the dogs [...] I can remember the ventral cavity. Then they cut out the heart and gave it to my six-year-old brother, still beating, he claimed ever afterwards, or still twitching, and he went dancing home singing: 'We've got the heart! We've got the heart!' So we cooked it up with a bit of flour, and the German au pair girl left the next day."

Johnson describes his exhilaration at demonstrating in favour of hunting together with eighty thousand hearty members of the Countryside Alliance and concludes that "hunting is best for the deer". [66]

During a celebrity England-Germany game of football, Johnson is caught on film making a twenty-yard charge designed to floor a German player by sinking his head into the player's stomach—a possessed move which, had he been a professional player, would have led to him being sent off the pitch or worse. The film footage records a rugby tackle in a game of soccer of a gratuitous and almost deranged violence.

Such a propensity for violence inevitably has to colour his political thinking. In an article for the right-wing *Daily Telegraph* in favour of Britain's nuclear weapons system, Johnson blusters, "If we want to be taken seriously we have to defend ourselves."

He continues: "You could not accuse us of lacking a historic martial spirit. It is a fact that of the roughly 200 countries in the world today, Britain has at one time or other invaded or conquered 178 of them." Johnson then adds with a dismissive contempt: "The only people to escape are places like Luxembourg."

"There is no other country" he adds proudly, "that comes close to that record of belligerence; not the Americans, not the French, not even the Romans."

This nationalistic mind-set of the football hooligan is then extended to justify spending £169 billion on Trident on the grounds that, by getting rid of it, Britain would be, in the view of this backward-looking imperialist, "denuding itself of its most important weapon".[67]

The arguments against the retention of Britain's "most important weapon", ominously lurking in a Scottish loch at Faslane, are well rehearsed, but not the least of them are the dangers inherent in Trident's maintenance as dramatically revealed by the whistle-blowing submariner William McNeilly, or to give him his full title, Engineering Technician Submariner for the UK's Trident II D5 Strategic Weapons System. McNeilly has shown that Britain's nuclear weapons system is poorly maintained, accident-prone, a health hazard and essentially a potential suicide bomb—a suicide bomb the consequences of which are unthinkable.[68]

Johnson, however, entertains the belief that the shambolically dangerous Trident is necessary for Britain's "global authority"—a belief that many would regard as delusional since Trident is not only strategically useless but it could also end up bestowing on Britain the same global kudos that the Chernobyl nuclear catastrophe gave the Russian Federation.

Johnson's propensity for violence goes back to his schooldays. His school newspaper, the *Eton Chronicle*, echoed the anti-Vietnam war chant when noting the violence which Alexander Boris Johnson displayed while he was playing the Eton Wall Game: "Hey! Hey! ABJ! How many Oppidans did you kill today?"[69]

Johnson was, according to his biographer, Andrew Gimson, "intensely proud of his achievements at school and loved being a leader there".

The Eton College tradition was that when you left the school you'd make an entry in the College Leaving Book. There was room for a comment and a Leaver Portrait of yourself taken by an approved school photographer.

On Johnson's departure, the College Leaving Book was found to contain "a large photograph of himself, with two scarves and a machine gun, together with an inscription about his determination to achieve 'more notches on my phallocratic phallus'".[70]

5

The Air of Lurking Violence

©Steve Bell 2010

BORIS JOHNSON'S PENCHANT for violence would soon find a further outlet in the initiation rites of Oxford's Bullingdon Club. Johnson was proud to be a member of the two hundred year old dining and drinking club and he would stand for its presidency. He was a keen participant in its excesses—raucous rituals described by an ex-member of it in the *Guardian*: "There's the air of lurking violence, and above all the sense that its members consider themselves above the law on such occasions."[71]

The club, whose youthful members like to dress up as if they belonged to a high-powered and gold-braided military elite, once enjoyed a "famously explosive dinner" at the White Hart near Oxford in 2005: "All the food and plates had been thrown everywhere and they were jumping on top of each other on the table like kids in a playground," recalled the pub's landlord Ian Rogers. The part he found strangest was that each time he confronted a member of the club, "they apologized profusely but offered absolutely no explanation".[72]

The Bullingdon Club is for plutocratic undergraduates who think nothing of spending £3,500 on its royal blue tailcoats with ivory lapels and canary yellow waistcoats—a livery which prompted Evelyn Waugh in *Brideshead Revisited* to describe the Bullingdon members as looking "like a lot of most disorderly footmen".[73]

The Bullingdon, described by Waugh in his novel *Decline and Fall*, published in 1928, as "baying for broken glass",[74] is still banned from meeting within a 15-mile radius of Christ Church. This stems from the time in 1927 when they smashed over 400 windows in the college's Peckwater Quadrangle. In Waugh's novel, the Bullingdon appears as the 'Bollinger', whose annual dinner was accompanied by "a confused roaring and a breaking of glass".

Waugh says, in a description that is now almost a hundred years old but which still applies:

It is not accurate to call this an annual event, because quite often the club is suspended for some years after each meeting. There is tradition behind the Bollinger; it numbers reigning kings among its past members. At the last dinner, three years ago, a fox had been brought in in a cage and stoned to death with champagne bottles.

What an evening that had been! This was the first meeting since then, and from all over Europe old members had rallied for the occasion. For two days they had been pouring into Oxford: epileptic royalty from their villas of exile; uncouth peers from crumbling country seats; smooth young men of uncertain tastes from embassies and legations; illiterate lairds from wet granite hovels in the Highlands; ambitious young barristers and Conservative candidates torn from the London season and the indelicate advances of debutantes; all that was most sonorous of name and title was there for the beano.

The current Minister of Foreign Affairs in Poland, Radek Sikorski formerly of Pembroke College, was surprised to be woken up in the middle of the night in his lodgings in Oxford's Walton Street and to be met by the sight of a marauding mob led by Boris Johnson, all whooping and chortling as Sikorski's room was trashed and his possessions destroyed by a welter of cricket bats and cricket stumps wielded with sadistic glee.

Sikorski sat up in his bed, bemused. "In the middle of the night," Sikorski recalls, "a dozen screaming figures burst into my room and demolished it completely."[75]

This was the Bullingdon Club's thuggish way of telling someone that they'd just been made a member and that, having endured this introductory ritual without complaint, they would now be privileged to do the same thing to new members and to enjoy themselves in similar fashion at their expense: to shred their clothes; to rip their books in half; to hurl their hi-fi systems to the ground while wine bottles were emptied onto a pile of their belongings in the centre of the room and while photographs of their girl friends were ripped up and decried.

In a *Guardian* article titled 'Young, rich and drunk', Barney Ronay writes: "Then there's the Bullingdon's committed and longstanding misogyny. It's not just the all-male exclusivity, more the tales of hiring strippers to preside at the initiation of new members at the annual breakfast. Plus the trapped, frantic and vaguely sexual energy of the whole thing. The Bullingdon is simply a no-go area for women. These are teenagers almost exclusively from an all-male boarding school background. It's no real surprise that some of the naive, hostile and retarded attitudes fostered there resurface at a university reunion. You just have to hope they grow out of it."[76]

Another stock-in-trade of the Bullingdon initiation rituals was for newly elected members to visit Bonn Square where Oxford's homeless congregate and to burn a £50 note in front of them by way of jeering at their misfortune.[77]

The Club is most noteworthy for its trashing of the restaurants that it has booked for its antics and then for its members to assume that they can exonerate themselves by throwing banknotes at the hapless, and possibly ruined, proprietors. As Hilaire Belloc had it in his *Cautionary Tales*:

Like many of the Upper Class
He liked the sound of broken glass.

Belloc could well have been thinking of the members of the Bullingdon Club. At one Club meal in 1987, attended by both Boris Johnson and David Cameron, someone—whose identity has never been properly established thanks to the Bullingdon rule of *omertà*—threw a large plant pot through the restaurant window.

The burglar alarm was activated and Oxford's police force duly descended on the dining club's chosen venue with sniffer dogs in tow. Six of the group were apprehended and spent the night at Cowley police station.

Cameron escaped but Johnson's attempt to evade the police by running off and crawling through a hedge in the Botanical Gardens failed and, by his own account, an overnight stay in a police cell reduced him to "a gibbering namby-pamby".

Cameron seems sheepish about his Bullingdon past. When asked by the TV interviewer Andrew Marr whether he was embarrassed by it, the then Tory leader replied: "Of course, desperately, very embarrassed about it". Johnson, however, seems proud of his Bullingdon membership and reputedly relishes hailing former members of the Club, so distinguished for its destructive binges, with a braying chant of "Buller! Buller! Buller!" which he expects to be reciprocated in a tribal bonding ritual.[78]

Johnson's defence of privilege is an enduring theme. In 1980, after extolling the virtues of private education he concluded: "So strain every nerve, parents of Britain, to send your son to this educational establishment (forget this socialist gibberish about the destruction of the State System). Exercise your freedom of choice because in this way you imbue your son with the most important thing, a sense of his own importance."[79]

The unfairness of the public schools' leech-like presence within the country's education system and their unwarranted charitable status—despite perpetuating an uncharitable class system—doesn't faze Johnson for a moment.

He admires and he serves economic elitism. Eighty per cent of those who funded his campaign for the office of mayor of London were from the financial sector—hedge-funders, private equity experts, financial service houses and multi-millionaire businessmen—something that may have weighed with Johnson when he later attacked the top tax rate for high earners and with his regarding "banker bashers" as deluded.

In November 2013 Johnson said the super-wealthy were "a put upon minority", and ludicrously described them as being "like Irish travellers and the homeless". In the same year the super-wealthy were to bag an average 14 per cent pay rise while the average wage rose by a paltry below-inflation 0.7 per cent.

"Since his first months in office," Sonia Purnell noted, "Boris's attitude towards the City and the super-rich has been at odds with his 'Mayor of the People' persona. As Simon Jenkins of the *Standard* tellingly puts it: "His defence of bankers' greed is Bullingdon morality, pure and simple."[80]

Johnson's more acute sister Rachel, a novelist, has commented on an infamous Bullingdon Club photograph (now strictly injuncted against publication) that features both her brother and Cameron: "It looks what it is, elitist, arrogant, privileged and of an age that would have little resonance with people on low incomes who didn't go to Eton."[81]

In the "overbearing arrogance embodied in these sub-Gainsborough postures—in the twittish clothing, the floppy hair and the almost luminous sense of false entitlement which radiate from these historic images"[82]—it's not hard to hazard a guess at their subsequent career paths.

In addition to Johnson and Cameron, the photograph also features a close friend of Boris Johnson's, one Darius Guppy—a man who, shortly after leaving University, was to embark upon a criminal career, and a man who is also widely suspected to have led Johnson himself—given Johnson's toleration of violence—into criminality.

As Andrew Gimson, put it: "No scandal, or alleged scandal, has pursued Boris for longer than the bizarre case of his tape recorded conversation with his Eton and Oxford chum Darius Guppy."[83]

Darius Guppy was aggrieved that his father, a partner in the Lloyd's insurance partnership, had lost much of his fortune together with the family home through a Lloyd's implosion in 1989. Massive claims made against some Lloyd's partners arrived all at once, most of them for the environmental damage caused by asbestos and by the Exxon Valdez oil spill.

Guppy felt that, in his words, "certain Lloyd's agents were in large measure responsible for what had happened, putting investors' money into dicey syndicates that would one day collapse under massive insurance claims".

Non-business folk such as Guppy's father were wilfully "lured into Lloyd's through a massive recruitment campaign, and while an avalanche of claims were hanging over the market".[84]

By way of revenge against the company which he held liable for his family's misfortune, Johnson's close friend Guppy planned an elaborate insurance fraud. In March 1990, Guppy arranged to have himself and his business partner, Ben Marsh, tied up in a room in the Halloran House Hotel in New York and to make it appear as if they'd been robbed of jewels worth £1.8 million.

Guppy recruited an Englishman called Peter Risdon to play the part of the robber. He and Marsh had met Risdon in London while Risdon was working for Counter Spy, purveyors of surveillance equipment in South Audley Street in Mayfair and where Risdon had boasted to them of his alleged criminal activities.

Guppy, Marsh and Risdon then devised a plan of action. Guppy and Marsh required Risdon, playing the part of the robber, to tie them both up and, for good measure, to fire a bullet into Guppy's pillow. Guppy and Marsh then made a successful claim against Lloyd's from which, having convinced Lloyd's loss adjustors that their losses were genuine, they profited handsomely—to the tune of £1.8 million.

The New York police however were suspicious, and when they questioned them both about the identity of the robber (whom Guppy and Marsh had falsely identified as being American), the NYPD investigating officer, detective Raymond Berke from the 17th Precinct, was alerted by the 'robber' allegedly asking both Guppy and Marsh to "Lie down on your front".

The normal American expression would have been "Lie face down". "Lie down on your front" was, the NYPD detective judged to be, what an Englishman would say.

There were other inconsistencies to do with the angle of the firing of the gun and its residual powder-marks which prompted the NYPD officer to wonder if this wasn't a sting staged by three Englishmen. He passed the details onto Scotland Yard.

As it happened, Peter Risdon, the 'robber', had also been having his own suspicions about Guppy, his partner in crime. Risdon believed that he, Risdon, was going to be set up and framed for the scam and the chances were that, instead of his sharing in the very considerable proceeds, he'd be languishing in a US jail while Guppy and Marsh, having cheated him, would escape to South America with their reward. Risdon therefore took the precaution of tapping into Guppy's telephone and recording his conversations.

At around the same time a *News of the World* journalist, Stuart Collier, had been making some inquiries in the course of writing a profile of Guppy for his paper. Guppy discovered to his consternation that Collier had been passing information about him to the New York police.

For the time being Guppy and Marsh, now back in England, had got away with it. Lloyd's had compensated them for the jewellery they'd claimed had been stolen and, understandably, they wished to continue getting away with it, so Guppy promptly turned for help to his old friend Boris Johnson, a fellow Old Etonian and a former Bullingdon Club member.

Guppy was determined to put Collier off the scent and decided that the best way to do this was by employing scare tactics. He informs Johnson that he's either going to beat Collier up himself or that he'll "hire some heavies to do it". He asks Johnson to find out Collier's address.

Instead of immediately discouraging his friend from this course of action, Johnson gives every indication of indulging Guppy's violent and criminal proclivities.

Unfortunately for both Guppy and Johnson, Risdon was recording the 21-minute call in which Johnson can be heard discussing how badly the journalist will be beaten up. Boris then agrees to use his journalistic contacts to supply Guppy with the address and telephone number of Stuart Collier, the journalist whose inquiries are threatening to expose Guppy and Marsh's fraudulent scam.

It is clear from what passes between Guppy and Johnson that this isn't the only conversation that they've been having about the subject and also that Johnson is at pains to agree to his friend's requests: "I got this bloody number for you. OK, Darry. I said I'll do it. I'll do it". Guppy is made aware that Johnson has been obliging him by putting out feelers amongst his newspaper contacts, four of whom have already indicated to Johnson that they will come back to Johnson with Collier's details.[85]

Johnson has to be familiar enough with English law to know that if anything happened to Collier, and if Johnson's part in it were to be discovered, then these exchanges would make him what is known in common law as an 'accessory before the fact'. In other words, it would make him criminally liable.

Consequently Johnson is at pains to impress upon Guppy how crucial it is that his, Johnson's, complicity be concealed. Guppy assures Johnson that his part in what both parties must assuredly know to be a crime will be totally untraceable to Johnson. Boris then seems less apprehensive and promises to provide Guppy with the prospective victim's address. Johnson's exact and incriminating words to Guppy caught on tape are: "I got this bloody number for you. OK Darry, I said I'll do it and I'll do it. Don't worry".

Once Guppy has been provided with the address he flies from Cape Town to London. Accounts now vary as to what exactly happened. Stuart Collier is apparently no longer a journalist and has gone to ground but, according to Guppy himself, he, Guppy, lay in wait for Collier, knocked the hapless journalist to the ground and covered him in manure. In other accounts, Collier is set upon and badly beaten.

It seems too that while Collier's offence in Guppy's eyes was the threat to expose the insurance fraud, Collier was also threatening to cast aspersions on Guppy's wife's past, thereby further fuelling Guppy's wrath.

Guppy angrily explains to Johnson that he wishes to avenge himself on a "tabloid scuzzbag" who has reduced his wife to tears. Collier, in Guppy's eyes, is doubly deserving of a serious bruising if not indeed a few broken bones. Guppy emphasises that it is "no worse than what happened to you in rugby". Johnson does not at any point demur nor does this Tory advocate of law and order take exception to the idea of two men conspiring to take the law into their own hands, nor to the idea that blood is imminently to be shed.

The taped conversation was recorded in the summer of 1990 at Guppy's then home in Chelsea. At the time of the phone call, Johnson was working for the *Daily Telegraph* in Brussels. Here is the transcript:

Johnson: If it got out . . .
Guppy: That he'd been beaten up.
Johnson: Beaten up, it would inevitably get back to the contact.

Johnson then says that he has used four contacts to track down information about Collier, but that he's worried one of them "might put two and two together, if he heard that this guy [Collier] had been beaten up..." Guppy interrupts him:

Guppy: But Boris there's absolutely no ******* proof: you just deny it. I mean, there's no proof at all ...
Johnson: Well yeah.
Guppy: I mean, you know, big deal. You're sitting in Brussels and the day it happens you're in Brussels, it's as simple as that.

Guppy repeatedly appeals to Johnson to have faith in him. At one stage Johnson replies in a slightly slavish tone: "I do have faith in you".

Guppy continues: "As far as I'm concerned, I have never told you what I require this number for. You do not know at all ... so you are totally off the hook". He adds: "You have nothing to fear. I give you my personal guarantee, OK, and my word of honour."

By the end of the conversation, Johnson says that he has the requested details and that he will divulge them. He is volunteering to do what he can to help, even though Guppy has spelled out the negative ways that Johnson's help will affect Collier's wellbeing. Guppy says: "He will probably get a couple of black eyes and a . . . a cracked rib or something."

Johnson expresses no real concern at all about the man's probable injuries. His sole concern is for his own back. Guppy repeatedly reassures him:

Guppy: We'll do it discreetly. That's all I require, just the address: the address and the phone number … all right? Now I guarantee you, you have nothing to worry about. [Slowly, emphatically] Believe me. All right? You have my personal guarantee. I've never let you down, all right?
Johnson: I got this bloody number for you. OK Darry, I said I'd do it and I'll do it. Don't worry.[86]

The reason for Peter Risdon's going public with the tape was that he found himself increasingly disillusioned by the duplicity of modern politicians and he'd decided that this, at least, would be one way of catching one meretricious MP in the act.

When in April 2009, to Johnson's discomfort, excerpts from Risdon's tape were aired for the first time as part of a *Dispatches* TV programme called "The Trouble With Boris", Johnson squirmed and swallowed hard and then attempted to brush it off by saying: "It was all a bit of a joke. It was all rather harmless. It was just Darry [Guppy's nickname]."[87]

When confronted by the filmmaker Michael Cockerell with more extensive extracts from the recording for a BBC programme, *The Irresistible Rise of Boris Johnson*, Boris again tried to laugh it off, but could be seen to be shifting his physical position in obvious anguish. He claimed that the sound-clips "were taken out of context" and he insisted twice "nothing eventuated from that conversation".[88] But this latter was not true.

Asked how he felt while listening to the recording, Johnson briskly snapped that it was "a load of old cobblers". But it wasn't. The recording was authentic and while Johnson was claiming on camera that "nothing eventuated" from the call, Guppy himself was, and is, in no doubt about what he did to Collier once he'd been supplied with his whereabouts by Johnson.

In an interview which Guppy gave to the *Daily Mail* on his release from prison, Guppy boasted: "I knocked him [Stuart

Collier] to the ground and tipped slurry on his head."[89]

The *Daily Mail*'s telegraphic headlines made it clearer still: "Boris Johnson's friend Guppy, 49, says he flew from Cape Town to London to exact revenge on man. He took exception to an article he believed 'humiliated' his wife, Patricia. Guppy is an old friend of the Mayor of London and of Earl Spencer. In 1993 he was jailed for organising a faked jewel heist for £1.8m insurance."[90]

Elsewhere Guppy speaks of giving a tabloid journalist "the hiding which most of us secretly admit such people deserve". Asked if he has any regrets, Guppy responds: "Only that I was never able to finish the job."[91]

Later in an article in the *New Statesman* Guppy would confirm in greater detail that, despite Johnson's denials that anything had happened and despite his alternative claim that in any case it was "all a joke", he, Guppy, had most assuredly attacked Collier:

"Having discovered his [Collier's] address and flown into London from South Africa where I live, I waited for him to emerge from his house, chased him, and then, having knocked him to the ground, emptied over his head a sack of horse manure rendered slurry by the addition of bottled water—a concoction made possible courtesy of Hyde Park Riding School and the springs of Évian."

"The aim had been not to hurt him but to humiliate him as he had sought to humiliate my wife. And humiliate him is exactly what I did, in front of his neighbours who had poured out on to the street at the sound of his screams."

Guppy claims he also had two "accomplices, who did not touch him", whom he said had recorded the event, but did not upload it onto the internet.[92]

Confronted again by the details of this affair while he was running for the office of mayor of London, Boris Johnson made a slightly different attempt to brush it off by saying of his old friend that he lived by "the Homeric code of honour, loyalty and revenge". But his attempt to dignify what was a squalid and brutal chain of events by bamboozling his interlocutor with rarefied classical references was an obvious ploy.

He and Guppy were not Hector and Achilles in some new Trojan War fighting the forces of darkness. Instead Guppy was a fraudster soon to be jailed for five years for staging a fake jewel heist in an insurance scam and, as the tape recording makes abundantly clear, the complicit and colluding Johnson was a spineless pander, colluding with Guppy in what was quite evidently a criminal enterprise, namely causing someone grievous bodily harm.

Johnson was prepared to do Guppy's dirty work in order to allay Guppy's fear about being found out in a serious fraud. Had Guppy "finished the job", as he euphemistically put it, and had the journalist, Stuart Collier, been murdered, Johnson, being in common law an accessory before the fact, would have faced a hefty jail sentence.

Johnson, helpfully providing Guppy with Collier's details, had no means of knowing how far Guppy would go, but Johnson would doubtless have been familiar with his fellow Bullingdon Club member's frequent boast of being a "potential psychopath".[93]

Furthermore, Johnson would also have been aware of his great friend's temper. As Guppy wrote in his memoir: "I had a temper that I could never ignore and that it seemed I was quite capable of hurting someone if I felt they deserved a beating."[94]

On 24 March 2013, Boris Johnson appeared on the BBC's *Andrew Marr Show* expecting the usual safe PR interview about his aims and achievements, only to receive the exact opposite from Marr's stand-in host, Eddie Mair:

"What does that say about you, Boris Johnson?" Mair challenged after he'd raised the Guppy affair, "Wanting to be a part of someone being physically assaulted? You're a nasty piece of work, aren't you?"

Quite how someone who had got themselves so uncritically involved in the Guppy affair could then present themselves as being in favour of law and order in London while he was standing for mayor or indeed as a Tory MP for Henley and later Uxbridge is a mystery. The answer can only be someone of breathtaking arrogance and entitlement, or of what Aristotle called "an incontinent personality".

Given that, according to Andrew Gimson, Johnson is prepared to lie about almost anything if it suits his purpose (making, for example, repeated promises of marriage to someone whom he wishes merely to seduce and abandon[95]) his flustered denials of any involvement in the Guppy affair cannot be taken seriously. Elsewhere when he has been cornered about the tape, Johnson has admitted to this much:

"Darius and I had a long rambling conversation that took in many heroes, many military heroes of ours, Rommel…"

This excuse prompted a scathing comment on a socialist blog: "Rommel! So there you have it, Tory candidate name-checks Nazi as military hero—probably he'd dismiss it as just 'richly comic' but Nazis, to rich and right-wing racists like Johnson are not funny. Even when they play the fool."[96]

To Johnson's considerable chagrin, the Guppy scandal will not go away. When on the TV programme *Have I Got News for You*, Ian Hislop of *Private Eye* took Boris Johnson to task over his part in providing Guppy with an address whilst knowing that he might be enabling a crime to be committed, a visibly paling and snarling Johnson stared back at Hislop and seethed apoplectically.

Hislop recalls, "He was absolutely livid because I brought up the Darius Guppy tape, which I found immensely funny. He was in a terrific strop and blustered about an elephant trap."[97]

Johnson's intemperate reaction prompts the inevitable question: if nothing had 'eventuated' from the taped conversation and if indeed it was all a joke, then why be so upset by it? But of course it wasn't so innocent after all, and darker deeds were most assuredly afoot.

6

Castrating Europe

©*Peter Brookes 2016*

MANY OF BORIS JOHNSON'S LIES are harmless. He was, for example, asked by *Who's Who* to provide a hobby for his entry. He chose 'scuba-diving'. His first wife, Allegra Mostyn-Owen, pointed out that scuba diving was in fact her hobby, "which he was rather bad at—I did laugh. He uses up his oxygen too fast. I don't think he ever repeated it [scuba diving], so it was a bit of a fib, but kind of vaguely revealing".[98] Other lies however have had a more far-reaching effect. His lie about Jacques Delors and the

Maastricht Treaty wishing to castrate every independent country in Europe was splashed all over the front page of the *Sunday Telegraph*, but was then also translated into Danish at a moment when Denmark was caught up in the thick of a referendum about its place in Europe.

Johnson's article was to be widely reprinted in Denmark's newspapers. "My boast," Johnson proclaimed (with the requisite helping of self-deprecation), "and I make it in the confidence that no one gives a monkey's, is that I probably did contribute to the Danish rejection of Maastricht."[99]

It would seem that this was in fact the case. Before the article's appearance, opinion polls had suggested a narrow vote in favour of the Maastricht treaty on 2 June; afterwards they pointed to a narrow vote against.

Johnson rejoiced in his article's impact and now recalls: "With less than a month until the Danish referendum [...] the story was seized on by the No campaign. They photocopied it a thousandfold. They marched the streets of Copenhagen with my story fixed to their banners. And on June 2nd, a spectacularly sunny day, they joyously rejected the Treaty and derailed the project. Jacques Delors was not the only victim of the disaster; the aftershocks were felt across Europe and above all in Britain."[100]

In his book on Brexit, Denis MacShane has outlined the origins of Johnson's duplicitous threats to Europe and the hidden hand behind them:

"Boris Johnson and the other editors who for more than two decades have published myths, lies and propaganda about Europe could only have acted thus if they had the blessing of their proprietors." And, adds MacShane, it explains why Conrad Black, the neo-conservative Canadian owner of the *Spectator* and the *Telegraph*, "appointed Boris Johnson editor of the *Spectator* to ensure that Britain's most virulent but very clever anti-European propagandist was at the centre of the London press hostility against the EU."[101]

David Usborne, the Brussels correspondent of the *Independ-*

ent said of Johnson: "Boris understood immediately what the *Telegraph* wanted to hear and he delivered in spades. Once he got his confidence up he started firing every torpedo he had at the Commission. He was writing things without really believing in his heart what he was writing. He would take something that might make a few paragraphs and turn it into an atomic bomb. I don't really think he was pursuing a political agenda about Europe, I think he was pursuing his own future."[102]

Johnson is also credited with having created a future for UKIP, widely regarded as a retrograde addition to the British body politic:

"A spokesman from UKIP (United Kingdom Independence Party), which campaigns for Britain's withdrawal from the EU, says that Boris's writings 'helped to pave' the way for the rise of his party. Its leader Nigel Farage goes further by saying that before Boris made them a fashionable cause, Eurosceptic leanings were 'something that would only be shared amongst close personal friends. They were a minority pursuit.' After Boris, there were few on the Right who did not join the Eurosceptic bandwagon."[103]

Speaking of his self-serving antics in Brussels on the BBC programme Desert Island Discs in October 2005, Johnson told his listeners: " ... everything I wrote from Brussels, I found was sort of chucking these rocks over the garden wall and I listened to this amazing crash from the greenhouse next door over in England as everything I wrote from Brussels was having this amazing, explosive effect on the Tory party, and it really gave me this rather weird sense of power."[104]

Johnson's rapacious power-hunger brings to mind a salutary thought from *The Restaurant at the End of the Universe* by Douglas Adams: "It is a well-known fact that those people who most want to rule people are, ipso facto, those least suited to do it ... anyone who is capable of getting themselves made President should on no account be allowed to do the job."

It is worth noting in passing that the "explosive" story which

Johnson filed ("Delors Plans to Rule Europe") wasn't actually his own. It was merely an exaggerated version of a story which had been filed by John Palmer, the *Guardian*'s Brussels correspondent, a few days before. Palmer still feels "incensed" by Johnson's plagiarism and by his distortion of the facts.

"... as a journalist he [Johnson] is thoroughly irresponsible, inventing stories. Just before the Danish referendum, I wrote a story about Delors' thinking on the next stages of political integration in the *Guardian*. Boris came up to me when it appeared and asked whether I'd seen the relevant documents. He then rewrote my story and completely distorted it to say 'Delors Plans to Rule Europe'.

"In fact, it was all about mere ideas on majority voting, more powers for the European Parliament and that sort of thing. Then what happened was that the extreme Europhobes in Denmark took Boris's inaccurate version and produced it as a leaflet. Whenever he was challenged about his rubbish, he would never actually defend his corner, he just blamed London, he was quite shameless. But what Boris wrote was taken as gospel by the zealots. It fuelled the whole UKIP phenomenon."

A Boris supporter pointed out to Sonia Purnell: "The irony is that Boris is a pro-European at heart. So why did he do it? Pure opportunism. It made him feel powerful."[105]

Johnson may still, somewhat deludedly, be thought of in some quarters as a 'national treasure' but he is hardly thought of as one in Liverpool. Shortly after a much-loved Liverpudlian taxi-driver, Ken Bigley, who had courageously been bringing humanitarian aid from Liverpool to Iraq, was kidnapped by al-Qaeda and publicly decapitated in 2004, Johnson commissioned and published a peculiarly tasteless leader in the *Spectator*.

It was a sneering, class-ridden article by Simon Heffer that was signally devoid of empathy and which spitefully accused Liverpudlians of wallowing in their "victim status". Liverpool, Boris Johnson's *Spectator* declared, was "hooked on grief and likes to wallow in a sense of vicarious victimhood".

The article went on to criticise the way in which Liverpool people had reacted to the capture and murder in Iraq of Ken Bigley. It accused them of "mawkish sentimentality" in their distraught reaction to the execution of the Liverpool charity worker at the hands of psychotic killers.

The *Spectator*'s leader was, by any standards, gratuitously vile and Johnson's elitist and snobbish hand in the piece was apparent: "The extreme reaction to Mr Bigley's murder is fed by the fact that he was a Liverpudlian. A combination of economic misfortune ... and an excessive predilection for welfarism have created a peculiar and deeply unattractive psyche among many Liverpudlians."[106]

In an increasingly tense situation the wretched Johnson was then prevailed upon by his then party leader, Michael Howard, to apologise to the people of Liverpool—Howard being anxious not to lose Liverpool's Tory vote, in addition to him having been a long-term supporter of Liverpool's football team.

Johnson was reluctantly bundled off to Liverpool unclear as to how he should address the city. He would gracelessly nickname this ill-starred venture 'Operation Scouse-Grovel' but he was soon to realise that he was on a very sticky wicket and his awkward insincerity was soon scented out, by no less a person than Ken Bigley's brother.

When Johnson appeared on the BBC's Roger Phillips radio show in Liverpool and when, after a mealy-mouthed apology, Johnson foolishly insisted that he could "not retract the broad thrust of the article", Paul Bigley saw a red mist and came onto the programme to tell Boris: "You're a self-centred, pompous twit, even your body language on TV is wrong. You don't look right, never mind act right. Get out of public life!"

As Sonia Purnell remarked: "It was a rare occasion when a member of the public has taken Boris on and for a moment he looked shaken by it. 'That was a difficult moment—it stripped a coat off him,' echoed Quentin Letts, one of the press pack following Boris. 'It hasn't happened much'".[107]

But the *Spectator*'s unwarranted attack on Liverpool at such a time had been an extraordinarily revealing error of judgment on Johnson's part. He was saying, in effect, that the Bigley family and their grief did not matter beside an opportunity for Johnson to take a whole city to task for its feelings—feelings that Johnson couldn't and wouldn't appreciate given his inability to empathise with those whom, deep down, he felt disdainfully superior to.

"Shortly after al-Qaeda murdered Liverpudlian Ken Bigley in Iraq in 2004, by cutting off his head, Boris Johnson thought this would be a good time to attack the people of Ken's home city," wrote the author of the blog, *Organized Rage*. [108]

Sonia Purnell has made a particularly unsettling observation of her biography's subject: "He never laughs. Real laughter involves losing control, and Boris never does that."

Interestingly it's been shown that the more someone practises self-deception, the less likely they are genuinely to laugh.[109]

Rather than his expressing real laughter, Johnson instead opts for becoming a mere character. In his book *Being a Character* the psychoanalyst Christopher Bollas defines a 'character' as being someone whose deeper self is empty, or angry, or socially alienated.[110]

An Oxford contemporary who was interviewed by Sonia Purnell but who didn't wish to give her name said of him: "Boris showed that he was not loyal, that he does not have many real friends, as it is all about him. People were wary of him. He was always fudging everything. So I could see that Boris wouldn't really keep friends because he doesn't have principles. I knew that bumbling thing was an act—he has a real 'economical with the actualité' persona."[111]

Michael Binyon, the *Times* correspondent in Brussels, remembers attending the daily press conferences and being asked by a veteran French journalist present as she indicated Boris Johnson, this shambolic 17-stone British fabulist, "Qui est ce monstre?"[112]

Curiously, Johnson's former partner in crime, Darius Guppy,

has recently stepped forward to comment on the great issue of the day. Margaret Thatcher once said of Boris Johnson: "He's my favourite journalist"[113] but, writing in the *New Statesman*, Guppy chastises his friend for his reciprocal love of Thatcher: " ... the Boris I knew well at school and university shared with me a love of classics—in particular, the heroes of the classics and the primal values that moved them. While such a world-view is compatible with a love of country, I do not see Achilles or Hector bowing before such a patently ignoble, money-worshipping and ultimately unpatriotic philosophy as Thatcherism."

"Let Johnson and Michael Gove," concludes Guppy, "also challenge Washington and Goldman Sachs and then we will see how brave they really are."[114]

There is no likelihood of this and, as regards Thatcher, there is little chance of Johnson being wrenched away from her effigy or cold-hearted legacy. According to Johnson his wife Marina "found him sobbing in the street over Thatcher's downfall, claiming it was as if someone had shot Nanny".[115]

7

A Couple of Immature Schoolboys

©Steve Bell 2010

COMPARE FOR A MOMENT the difference between a European and a British mind-set: on Thursday 25 February 2016, the European Parliament voted for an EU-wide arms embargo against Saudi Arabia in protest against its bombardment of its southern neighbour, Yemen, and the wilful killing of civilians and the bombing of schools.

This may be set against David Cameron's visit to the weapons manufacturer, BAE Systems, boasting of his efforts to sell "brilliant things" such as Eurofighter Typhoons to Saudi Arabia on the very day the European parliament voted for an arms embargo.[116]

It is unlikely that any such vote would ever be passed in the British Parliament as it's presently constituted—although it might if Jeremy Corbyn were elected as Prime Minister.

Corbyn has distanced himself from Boris Johnson's Brexit with its 'little Englander' mentality and its espousal of isolationism, its pride in past imperial power, and its free-market capitalism unfettered by government regulations, especially by what it calls 'foreign governments' in Brussels, and its reluctance to adopt the EU's human rights legislation.

Corbyn said that he wished to reform the EU from within and to make it a more socialist bloc. Writing in the *Guardian* he said: "Labour will be running a positive campaign for the real change we need: to unite opposition to austerity and build a Europe of sustainable growth, jobs and social justice."[117] And in a speech on 14 April 2016 to Labour supporters, Jeremy Corbyn made it clear that leaving the European Union would, in his words, "lead to a bonfire of rights".

"Britain needs to stay in the EU as the best framework for trade, manufacturing and cooperation in 21st century Europe. Tens of billions of pounds worth of investment and millions of jobs are linked to our relationship with the EU, the biggest market in the world. In contrast to four decades ago, the EU of today brings together most of the countries of Europe and has developed important employment, environmental and consumer protections."

Corbyn continued by describing how "EU membership has guaranteed working people vital employment rights, including four weeks' paid holiday, maternity and paternity leave, protections for agency workers and health and safety in the workplace". And he added that, "being in the EU has raised Britain's environmental standards, from beaches to air quality, and protected consumers from rip-off charges".

Despite the British media's demonization of Corbyn, he remains that *rara avis*, a decent, honest and principled politician, whereas Boris Johnson's Brexit agenda was negative, doom-laden, and led by an unsettling cabal of the self-seeking.

Were any further proof needed of Johnson's amoral and dishonest opportunism it can be gathered from his welcoming party for the phone-hacking mogul Rupert Murdoch to Murdoch's new headquarters at London Bridge.

Sweeping aside the carnage caused by this scheming and conniving monopolist who controls the Fox network and News Corp, and who holds dominion over much of western media, Johnson chose to greet him with emetic effusions of flattery as a "wise, benevolent, and far-sighted monarchical figure".[118]

In Australia Murdoch was notorious for encouraging door-stepping techniques amongst his journo hacks that drove their victims to suicide. [119] Ghoulish and necrotic the elderly leopard may be, but he hasn't changed his spots and he now had the added comfort of Boris Johnson kowtowing to him.

Anthony Hilton revealed in the *London Evening Standard* a conversation he once had with Rupert Murdoch about the UK's membership of the European Union. Hilton asked Murdoch why he was so opposed to the EU. "That's easy," Murdoch replied, "when I go into Downing Street, they do what I say; when I go to Brussels they take no notice."[120]

The thought of Johnson in Downing Street being the lickspittle of his undemocratic and unseen paymaster, Rupert Murdoch, is alarming, but Johnson is capable of being just that. When there was a move by his friends to help him to become the proprietor of the *Spectator* as well as being its editor, Johnson commented: "Still if the owner is someone other than myself, I am ready to be Vichy-like. I am prepared to praise and flatter shamelessly."[121]

As well as, by his own admission, being prepared to praise and flatter, he is, thanks to a constitutionally competitive nature, prepared also to give the most outlandish of rumours an airing should it suit his political rivalry. The following story appeared in the *Spectator*'s gossip column credited to 'Steerpike' and it was tellingly positioned beneath a photograph of Johnson. Its headline read: "Revealed: Boris Johnson's Piers Gaveston porkies".

Steerpike continued:

"With Lord Ashcroft's claim in today's *Daily Mail* that David Cameron once enjoyed intimate relations with a dead pig, talk has soon turned to which unnamed Tory MP was the source of the story.

"With the incident allegedly taking place at an initiation ceremony for the Piers Gaveston dining society—which is named after Edward II's alleged male lover—it has been suggested that one of Cameron's Oxford university contemporaries could be the source. While Steerpike is yet to discover which MP is behind the Ashcroft tale, Mr S. couldn't help but remember that one Tory MP previously got himself into trouble for telling porkies concerning Piers Gaveston."[122]

The implication couldn't be clearer. The *Spectator*, no longer edited by Johnson but reliably on the inside track of Tory antics, confidently implied that the rumourmonger was Johnson.

By all accounts Johnson loathes his rival, David Cameron, to distraction, as he considers him his intellectual inferior who by a fluke has cheated Johnson of the job that he considers is rightfully his, and this rivalry can have infantile manifestations from the circulation of slanderous rumours to brawling physically.

At David Cameron's annual summer garden party for Westminster journalists, Cameron revealed the following to the veteran political journalist Michael Crick:

"Earlier that week, Cameron explained, the pair [Johnson and Cameron] had sat facing each other in the Cabinet Room, with Johnson outlining his plans for London and requests for help. Then, as Cameron started responding, with help from a sheaf of briefing papers, Johnson leant across the table. 'What's all this? Let's see!' he cried as he tried to snatch the documents from the PM's grasp. Cameron held on to his precious notes, and for a few moments the two Conservative politicians wrestled and tugged for supremacy across the cabinet table, like a couple of immature schoolboys. Officials looked on in astonishment. It was hugely undignified, yet hugely symbolic."[123]

In another account of this rivalrous brawl, James Kirkup of the *Daily Telegraph* adds a salient detail:

"The PM has a briefing paper that reveals the most he's prepared to give Boris. Boris wants to see it. The PM refuses. Boris tries to grab it. The PM snatches it away. The Prime Minister and the Mayor of London end up wrestling on the floor trying to seize the paper. And the vital detail is that each man tells the story that he got the paper. Even in a slightly juvenile squabble, they both want people to know that they won over the other."[124]

According to Crick, "Johnson has spent his life pretending he's rather more upper class than he really is, calculating, perhaps, that the British public love a toff, especially if he's unthreatening, dishevelled and bumbling." However, Crick adds: "Cameron has stronger links to the British aristocracy" and the somewhat ungainly Johnson resents Cameron's svelte air of effortless superiority.

In vying for position in their hierarchical imaginings, David Cameron boasts of having been born with two silver spoons in his mouth while Boris Johnson arrogates to himself a supposed descent from the porcine Hanoverian George II.

As Kirkup pointed out, "Europe may well decide the duel between the Prime Minister and the Mayor once and for all. Imagine how that plays out now. Mr Cameron beat the star of stars to the top prize—yet Mr Johnson has never seemed to acknowledge that victory, much less respect it. He can rarely resist the chance to tweak the tail of the man he sometimes describes as 'Cameron Minor', a little chap from one of the lower forms".

His sister, Rachel, is even more overt in expressing Clan Johnson's militant lack of deference to Mr Cameron. Speaking to the BBC for a documentary, she described her brother's relationship with the Prime Minister and his "sense of superiority" over Mr Cameron. "When they're together it's rather sweet, because David Cameron—even though he's taller—looks at Boris as if he's still head boy at Eton. Remember, Cameron was two years younger—the young pup."[125]

In turn, Cameron's rivalry is fuelled by the fact that, according to a recent memoir by the former cabinet minister, David Laws, he, Cameron, is "petrified" of Johnson. Laws' book reveals that "the prime minister fretted [...] about the EU referendum, saying that 'the only person this will help is Boris Johnson, who is clearly after my job'."[126]

Enter the Gaveston pig onto this combative stage, pursued by journalists, gossip columnists and comedians world-wide. Was it Johnson who, green with jealousy, latched onto rumours of necrophiliac bestiality and gave the story currency?

Whoever it was, the pig allegation spread and it became widely known as Pig-gate. Under the headline "Bacon Smutty" the *Sun* wrote: "Claims David Cameron put his privates in a dead pig's mouth went viral yesterday with mock-ups of the PM in swine-related activities. He posed with a live hog last year."

Pig masks instantly proved a runaway bestseller, popular with those demonstrating outside Tory gatherings against the Tory Party's austerity cuts—especially if it was known that the hapless Cameron would be in attendance.

The *Sun* story was followed up by another headline: "Who let the hogs out? PORKERGATE: Downing Street launches 'Ham Cam' probe" in the course of which another finger of suspicion was pointed at Johnson.[127]

The lyricist Tony Bicât caught the country's mood of incredulous hilarity in his "Song for Europe" in which he has Johnson declare: "My todger's toured the parish, but at least I've kept it out of swine."

It's not known how gratifying Johnson found the fruits of the leak, but his peddling of the rumour, if it was him, has not been entirely beneficial and inevitably it rebounded. The comedian Bob Mortimer tweeted #AskBoris, Johnson's twitter feed, "You've got a bit of a piggy face. Was David ever tempted?"

Very much more seriously, given his constitutionally confron-

tational nature, Johnson has declared himself to be wholehearted-
ly in support of the Trident nuclear missile programme and of its
refurbishment at the lunatic cost of £169 billion.[128]

His reasons for clinging onto such an unconscionable weapon
that can never be used are unconvincing but the thought of a
person such as himself having any kind of say in the firing of any
missile, let alone a nuclear one, is beyond alarming. Johnson, after
all, is a man who, when out campaigning in the UK, hasn't known
which county he was in, whether in Gloucestershire or Wiltshire,
and upon being told which county it was, frothed idiotically:
"Gloucestershire? I get more confident on that sort of thing
towards the end of a visit."[129]

Imagine this cross between a Teletubby and Dr Strangelove
shouting 'Fire!' down a nuclear hotline to Faslane without
knowing which country he was aiming to obliterate.

In their wishful talk of how Boris will "save us" if he becomes
Prime Minister, some Tories, according to the *Economist*, talk of
"weaponising Boris" in order that he can rally their fractured
party and lead them and himself into Downing Street.

But a weaponised Boris Johnson with his finger hovering
over the nuclear button as its bumbling owner scrambles for a
headline grabbing *bon mot* with which to cheer up his audience, is
not a reassuring thought.

Perhaps nothing can better demonstrate Johnson's wrong-
headed and ill-constituted perversity than this quote from his TV
series *The Dream of Rome*, in which he indulges in a peculiarly off-
target revulsion for the early Christians:

"In their suicidal behaviour, in their belief in an afterlife, and
in their rejection of the values of the culture in which they found
themselves, the early Christians evoke early comparisons with
Islamic suicide bombers of today."[130]

Nothing in the behaviour of early Christians warrants such a
comparison of course. Johnson has allowed his naive infatuation
with the swaggering atrocities of ancient Rome to cloud his TV
scholarship.

A cursory look at the works of Irenaeus, Celsius, Clement of Alexandria, Athanasius or Origen (given their accounts of the conduct of early Christians before Christianity was ruined after being commandeered by Rome's Emperor Constantine) would reveal a revolutionary spirit that was communalist, almost wholly vegetarian, anti-authoritarian, and pacifist for its first three hundred years.

The early Christians valued sharing; they despised economic inequality and they told truth to power. They weren't suicide bombers and they certainly weren't Tories either.

In the untiring cause of Brand Boris's aggrandisement, in 2014 Johnson produced a potboiler and cuttings job on Winston Churchill of which Nick Cohen would write in the *Spectator*:

"Rather rashly, Boris Johnson published *The Churchill factor: How one man made history* last year. It was without historical merit, or intellectual insight, but Johnson did not intend readers to learn about Churchill. The biography was not a Churchill biography but a Johnson campaign biography, where we were invited to see our hero as Winston redux.

"Johnson believes in the advance of Johnson. That's all there is. There's nothing else. Most politicians, and many of the rest of us, are ambitious, of course. But politicians normally hope to advance a cause as they advance themselves. Johnson would have you believe that he is breaking with the establishment, risking all, because of his sincere conviction that we must advance the cause of saving Britain from the European Union.

"His colleagues do not believe him. Nicholas Soames called him a liar on Twitter yesterday. Jerry Hayes called him a 'copper-bottomed, hypocritical little shit'. The wonder of it is that they may have been understating the case for the prosecution."[131]

Nick Cohen was certainly understating the ex-Tory MP Jerry Hayes's lacerations. Hayes has described Johnson's "betrayal and a level of morality which would make an Algerian brothel owner blush. He is the embodiment of everything that the public despise about politicians. The effortless, wealthy ooze of entitlement, the laziness of mind and the incontinence of mouth, coupled with a psychotic drive to be Prime Minister."

Hayes added: "The public will be repulsed by his cynical opportunism. If this dreadful little man ever becomes leader of my party then I and so many moderates will move on. Many will say that Boris is his own worst enemy. Not while I'm about."[132]

During the Brexit campaign to leave the European Union, the ex-Prime Minister John Major described Johnson's misleading claims as "squalid". He regarded, for example, Johnson's notion that pulling out of the EU would allow Britain to spend more money on the National Health Service as particularly unconvincing and hypocritical since Johnson had long been advocating charging patients for NHS attendances. Major concluded that the NHS is about as safe with Johnson "as a pet hamster would be with a hungry python".

Not unsurprisingly, in almost any of Johnson's attempts to make a case for himself he overreaches. As mentioned, as a child Johnson was wont to declare that his ambition was to be "World King"[133] and this has now matured into what he confesses on occasion to being a "Messiah complex".[134]

Since historical figures with Messiah complexes often end up causing considerable pain and suffering (*vide* Charles Manson and Adolf Hitler) it might be worth bearing in mind Bishop Tutu's classic admonition, namely that "the one thing that we learn from history is that we don't learn from history".

That Johnson's own appreciation of history is partial, prejudiced and slapdash can be seen from his being outdone by Barack Obama in a controversy about the bust of Winston Churchill in the White House.

Angered by Obama's suggestion that Britain would be better off in Europe and that, in Obama's words, when it came to trade deals with the US, "the UK is going to be the back of the queue," if the UK were unwise enough to leave, Johnson retaliated by falsely claiming that Obama had removed the statue of Churchill from the White House upon his coming into office.

Johnson further suggested that Obama's action was "a symbol of the part-Kenyan president's ancestral dislike of the British Empire—of which Churchill had been such a fervent defender".[135]

Labour's shadow chancellor John McDonnell immediately called for Johnson to withdraw his comment, writing on Twitter: "Mask slips again. Boris part-Kenyan Obama comment is yet another example of dog whistle racism from senior Tories."

It may have been even more than that. It was a Taki-esque view of the president in which Johnson came close to suggesting that Obama is a Mau Mau fellow-traveller and also aligned himself with the loony right in the US, the so-called 'birthers', who dispute the fact that Obama was born in Hawaii and thus query his US citizenship and thereby try to disqualify him as their president for obviously racist reasons.

Churchill's grandson, Nicholas Soames, a Conservative MP backing the remain campaign, called Johnson's article "appalling" and said it was "inconceivable" that the wartime leader would not have welcomed Obama's views. He said Johnson was "unreliable and idle about the facts," claiming there was still a Churchill bust inside the White House.

A little later, without bothering to mention Johnson by name, President Obama also pointed out that Johnson's claim was simply untrue. Johnson hadn't done his homework. "Right outside the door of the Treaty Room," Obama said, "so that I see it every day—including on weekends when I'm going into that office to watch a basketball game—the primary image I see is a bust of Winston Churchill," he said. "It's there voluntarily because I can do anything on the second floor. I love Winston Churchill. I love the guy."[136]

8

Betrayal covered by a wink and a Smile

©Peter Brookes 2014

IF BORIS JOHNSON WERE TO DISAPPEAR off the face of the earth it would be hard to assess his legacy. He's perhaps most widely known for the so-called 'Boris Bikes' although, truth to tell, they're more accurately Barclays Bikes since they were paid for by Barclays Bank.

Johnson however has made off with Barclays' credit even though the idea for the bikes in fact belongs neither to him nor to Barclays Bank. As Nigel Cawthorne points out: "Before he had left office, Ken Livingstone had suggested a scheme of street-corner bike hire across the city. These became Boris Bikes and he was happy to take credit for them at the 2012 election."[137]

Despite his ostensible devotion to an environmentally friendly method of transport, Johnson's attempts to make London bike-friendly have failed:

"He came under criticism for his £4-million-a-mile cycling superhighways, which appeared to be nothing more than a line of blue paint that did nothing to protect their users. Indeed two people died at one junction in 2011."[138]

Rather more people have died due to London's notorious air pollution. The annual figure is some 9,500 premature deaths from respiratory diseases. Diesel particulates are now to be found in heart tissue.

In his campaign to be elected as mayor, Johnson had made air pollution an issue. Upon his election, however, London's mayor merely paid lip service to the issue and when confronted by a report on the subject, he held back its findings in order to give the impression that his mayoralty had achieved more than it had. It had achieved nothing.

The aggrieved author of the report said that City Hall had publicised its positive conclusions but significantly held back his finding that deprived schools were disproportionately affected by toxic air.[139]

Equally ill-starred was Johnson's purchase of a fleet of water cannon with which to repress his more demonstrative fellow-Londoners. Rashly, Johnson hadn't obtained clearance from Theresa May, the Home Secretary, whose prior approval should have been sought for their usage before Johnson spent £218,000 on the three second-hand Wasserwerfer 9000 machines which he had imported from Germany.

Johnson's purchase was under-researched. During a protest in Stuttgart in 2010 a German pensioner Dietrich Wagner had been left blind after being struck in the face by one of the cannons. In July 2015, Theresa May used a statement in the House of Commons to announce that she was turning down permission to use the devices on London's streets on the grounds of medical risk.

Furthermore, Ms May said that a review which she'd requested following Johnson's ill-considered acquisition found the cannons to be "dangerous, slow to deploy, and in some cases, not in complete working order".

She cited the age of the twenty-five-year-old machines and also her assessment that they would not be effective in a riot since advance notice of their use would be required and, furthermore, one of Johnson's machines needed no fewer than 67 repair operations. Johnson protested that the Government was "trying to clip my wings".[140]

After being criticised for spending £218,000 on three machines that couldn't be used, the Mayor then hid the embarrassing cannon from view.

A spokesman from Boris Johnson's office proved evasive in response to inquiries: "We have always been clear in public that we do not plan to comment on the location of the water cannon."

Thanks however to a BBC drone, the three mechanised follies of this all-round and near-spherical incompetent were discovered behind some hoardings in a south London holding bay, where they were now costing Mayor Johnson's office, and thus the taxpayer, an additional £1,740 a month.[141]

Understandably reluctant to continue paying for Johnson's costly incompetence, the incoming London mayor, Sadiq Khan, has announced the sale of the three second-hand water cannon that were prevented from ever being deployed.[142]

If Johnson is criticised he is liable to throw all his toys out of the pram, and if he is criticised in print, careless editors who are unaware that Johnson has a thin and notably humourless layer of skin have found themselves in receipt of vicious emails containing the message, "Fuck off and die".[143]

Likewise London taxi drivers, whom Boris is reputedly reluctant to tip, have found themselves subjected to similar levels of abuse. One London taxi driver publicly accused Johnson of failing to protect the city's black cab industry and he then shouted: "You're one of them mate. That's what you are. One of them."

Johnson shouted back with obstreperous viciousness: "Why don't you f**k off and die, why don't you f**k off and die—and not in that order." To the UK's national treasure the cab driver retorted: "Yeah bollocks, I hope you die." The exchange was filmed by a passer-by.[144]

In her biography, Sonia Purnell remarks unsettlingly: "The wife of one of his Bullingdon Club cohorts at Oxford 'would not speak about Boris, even off the record, as she is frightened of what he might do back. A lot of people are'."[145]

Within Brexit, Johnson must qualify as its Alpha Male but he overlooks the fact that the Tory Party's Alpha Male, Winston Churchill, called for a 'United States of Europe' shortly after the end of World War Two—Churchill's thought was that such a unity could provide a bulwark against any further devastation in Europe.

Brexit seeks to undo that unity and it's led by a cadre of conservatives who protest their love of country with a self-satisfied zeal and yet are unable to conserve the quality of its air, nor of its soil nor of its water. They are largely climate change deniers, advocates of nuclear power and nuclear weapons, proponents of genetically modified foods; those who give polluters a free rein if it 'serves the economy' and those who regard the defence of workers' rights as 'red tape'.

They will defend slave wages and the iniquities of 'zero hours contracts' and the privatisation of the National Health Service by rapacious US con men, while they fight with a low cunning to conserve a depraved British body-politic based upon an unconscionable disparity between untold wealth and unspeakable poverty and upon the idle values of transient celebrity.

When Christopher Hitchens adopted the United States as his country he boasted that it was "the only country based on an idea". But Europe can cap that being a whole continent based on an idea; possibly a set of rather good ideas.

In the words of Douglas Adams: "To be frank, it sometimes seems that the American idea of freedom has more to do with my freedom to do what I want than your freedom to do what you want. I think that, in Europe, we're probably better at understanding how to balance those competing claims, though not a lot."

In a recent fit of megalomania, Boris Johnson told the *Times* that he liked the idea of being a "plucky individual" standing up to the evils of the European Union. During the course of an interview, Johnson took pains to point out to his interviewer that *Spectre*, the most recent Bond movie, had been partly shot in his Mayor of London offices. "You are in the place," Johnson boasted, "where James Bond shoots the evil baddie who is hell bent on subverting democracy around the world through a supra-national organisation . . . I think there's a metaphor there."[146]

Ironically, given Johnson's desire to sprinkle himself with some James Bond stardust, someone mooted to play the next James Bond for real, namely the *Homeland* actor Damian Lewis, has blasted Boris Johnson for ruining London by handing it over to "the ultra-rich" and has criticised "the way they've taken up residency in London, the way that's been facilitated by our leaders and our politicians".

Lewis spoke of being "a proud Londoner," and accused Johnson of betraying his electoral promise to see that London wasn't turned into 'Dubai on Thames'. He continued: "I think London has changed and the heart of London is now inhabited by people with second, third, fourth homes, these super-rich, that class of people most of us don't know or come across."[147]

Having indulged super-rich speculators to buy up London as an investment rather than as a place to live, and thus threatening to alter London's character irreversibly, Johnson may, somewhat pitifully, persuade himself that he is a reincarnation of James Bond but perhaps there's a more apt metaphor to be found in his designs on William Blake, a man more inclined to empathise with

London's homeless than with its imported moguls.

Blake is buried in Bunhill Fields, a quiet haven in the centre of London which Boris Johnson—ever anxious to curry favour with City planners and profiteers—has shown himself determined to overshadow with an oppressive cluster of towering office blocks.

Blake's grave is the last resting place of a man who represented all that's best in the English spirit: a man who was horrified by the thought that "commerce settles on every tree". In the words of Niall McDevitt, the principal campaigner against the multi-storey development "He [Johnson] will be remembered as the Mayor who sold London's skyline."

McDevitt is not alone in his view. Writing in the *Observer*, Rowan Moore, the author of *Slow Burn City: London in the Twenty-First Century*, urges his readers to pity Johnson's successor as Johnson prepares to leave City Hall for they'll be "faced with ill-planned developments and vanity projects" in other words, "the bloated, bulging, light-blocking buildings" that Johnson leaves in his wake.

Moore points out that Johnson's phalanxes of towers that cast swathes of land "into almost permanent shadow" are ultimately "bad for business and bad for the London brand, promoting as it does both a speculative bubble and shoddy products".

Moore finally bids adieu to the much-vaunted classicist with these humiliating words: "Goodbye Boris. You have not left your city, as the Ephebic oath required of Athenians, more beautiful than you found it. You have been more like Nero, fiddling with vanity projects while it burns with clumsy overdevelopment."[148] Niall McDevitt wrote Johnson an open letter:

Dear Mayor,

I have started an AVAAZ petition to ask you to rethink your approval of the development at Bunhill Fields. It has been rushed through too fast. It is going to be one of your more unpopular decisions and may bounce back to haunt you as you begin to seek higher rungs of power than the one you already occupy.

A huge development going up at the side of this beloved green space and cultural heritage site will affect it negatively in numerous ways, some temporarily, some permanently. In the short term the noise and disruption will be a blight on this oasis of tranquillity. In the long term, the eleven and ten storey blocks will make Bunhill Fields colder and darker, oppressing the open space and ruining the skyline. Campaigners such as the Ancient Monuments Society have already warned you that the project is a 'bullying' and 'overwhelming' one".

Mayor Boris Johnson did not reply.

When Blake was thirteen he wrote a poem called "Song" about Phoebus who catches a bird in a silver net, shuts it in a golden cage and mocks its "loss of liberty". Later Blake would take the radical, anti-capitalist view that "where any view of Money exists Art cannot be carried on, but war only". In a couple of phrases, Blake thus nailed Bullingdon Toryism and its crass devotion to high finance and the military-industrial complex.

By contrast Johnson's loquacious, blustering claims to love England (and, via Brexit, to be protecting all that is best about it) are fraudulent; his monomaniac plans to foist himself further and further upon the body-politic are disturbing and to Blake aficionados Johnson's imminent plan to cast his oafish shadow upon Blake's mortal remains and to deprive them of light is akin to blasphemy.

While Boris Johnson may be a cult figure to some of his fellow Tories, for others his excesses are too much. The former Conservative MP and aide to Margaret Thatcher, Matthew Parris launched a scathing attack on the pro-Brexit mayor, denouncing him for alleged "dishonesty, vacuity, sexual impropriety and veiled homophobia".

"Somebody has to call a halt to the gathering pretence that if only you're sufficiently comical in politics you can laugh everything off," Parris wrote. "Incompetence is not funny. Policy vacuum is not funny. A careless disregard for the truth is not funny. Advising old mates planning to beat someone up is not funny. Abortions and gagging orders are not funny. Creeping ambition in a jester's cap is not funny. Vacuity posing as merriment, cynicism posing as savviness, a wink and a smile covering for betrayal ... these things are not funny."

Parris describes the mayor as a "lacklustre" politician, and claims that Johnson was unable to defend his recent claims about the European Union in front of the Treasury select committee in Parliament. Andrew Tyrie, the committee chair, accused Johnson of "exaggerating to the point of misrepresentation". It was not the case, as Johnson had maintained, that the EU had banned the British from recycling teabags nor that children under eight had been prevented from blowing up balloons; nor had the EU regulated on the size of coffins, and nor were EU regulations costing Britain £600m a day.

Parris added: "But there's a pattern to Boris's life, and it isn't the lust for office, or for applause, or for susceptible women, that mark out this pattern in red warning ink. It's the casual dishonesty, the cruelty, the betrayal; and, beneath the betrayal, the emptiness of real ambition: the ambition to do anything useful with office once it is attained." He added, for good measure: "Boris Johnson has killed the distinction between reality and satire."[149]

The writer Will Black quipped in a tweet addressed to the Mayor: "Hi @MayorofLondon do you think Matthew Parris should be beaten up for this?" Again, no reply from Johnson's office was forthcoming.

Hot on the heels of Parris, and clearly alarmed by the possibility that Johnson could become Britain's prime minister, the veteran political commentator, Nick Cohen, entitled an article for the *Guardian* 'Boris Johnson. Liar, conman—and prime minister?'

He warned: "It is easy to see how Boris Johnson could be prime minister by the autumn. 'Leave' wins, and David Cameron resigns. We already know that a majority of the 140,000 or so Conservative Party members, who will decide the government of a country of 64 million, back him. Give them the chance, and they will put him in Downing Street."

Cohen indicated that Johnson's attitude toward Europe has been entirely opportunistic. "Any man," Cohen says, "with a functioning sense of shame would have worried about his long record of supporting the EU. As late as February, Johnson was saying that leaving would embroil 'the government for several years in a fiddly process of negotiating new arrangements, so diverting energy from the real problems of this country'. And so it would. Elsewhere he acknowledged that we would not get free trade without accepting EU regulation and immigration."

Cohen points out: "The Mayor of London has been treated with woozy indulgence by the media. My supposedly hard-bitten colleagues have bought his persona as a lovable card, and ignored the emptiness beneath. But Britain may pay the price".[150]

However it's not just Britain that may pay the price, it's also Europe—if not the world. In its issue of 14 May 2016, the loyal Fraser Nelson, political editor of Johnson's former magazine, the *Spectator*, wondered what the future held for Johnson. He declared that "if the bookmakers are to be believed" Boris has "a Tory leadership campaign to assemble". Nelson added confidently, "He's currently red-hot favourite for the top job".[151]

Some Tory colleagues were however alive to the dangers of Johnson being in pole position as Premier. Amber Rudd MP, government Energy Secretary, said witheringly of him: "Boris is the life and soul of the party, but he isn't the man you want driving you home at the end of the evening."[152]

Anthony Wells, director of political polling at YouGov, wondered if Johnson's star was fading. He said it was impossible to know if his popularity would hold up if there were a serious prospect of him becoming prime minister. "It's fine being mayor of London going down the zipwire waving flags, but would that suddenly stop being funny if there was a chance of him having his finger on the nuclear button?"

©*Gerald Scarfe, Sunday Times 8/5/16*

9

The Murder of Jo Cox

©Steve Bell 2016—with apologies to Gustave Doré

WHEN CONFUCIUS WAS ASKED what he'd do first if he were called upon to rule a nation he replied: "I'd correct language. If language isn't correct, then what is said is not what's meant, and what ought to be done remains undone. Morals and art deteriorate and justice goes astray—and if justice should disappear then people will stand about in helpless confusion. So there must be no arbitrariness in what's said. It matters above everything."

"Careless talk costs lives" was a famous cautionary slogan during World War Two and it is no less true now. As the language about Britain's relation to Europe grew increasingly inflammatory in the run-up to the referendum, with bloviating Brexit tribunes calling for the "restoration of national sovereignty" by their stemming 'alien tides', and by their building draconian defences for our island borders to put paid to 'swarms' of refugees whose human cause was undermined by such reifying language designed to regard them as no more than invading insects, and as intemperate voices urged Britons to seize back control of their island nation, this headline appeared on 16 June 2016: 'British MP Jo Cox Murdered in Presumed Brexit-Related Attack'.[153]

A young Labour Party MP had been gunned down and stabbed by someone shouting "Britain First"—someone who, on being arraigned in court two days later would give his name as "Death to Traitors. Freedom for Britain".[154]

Jo Cox had held a senior position in Oxfam and she had leant successfully on the UK government to take in more Syrian refugees. Her concerns had led her to several of the world's most dangerous troublespots. She was by all accounts not in politics for the kudos nor for the cash, but just to do good in a needy and often wicked world and to do it with an impassioned altruism that those who knew her found quite exceptional. In a tribute a friend of hers, Martin Kirk, wrote that Jo Cox was "driven by an unambiguous desire to make life better for those battered and beaten and punished by this world".

She was just 41-years-old when she was murdered.

Her bereaved husband Brendan's immediate reaction was to say that mainstream politicians had been reinforcing the mindset of right-wing populists on immigration and that they had been "fanning the flames of resentment".[155] One blustering demagogue came immediately to mind.

Doreen Lawrence, the Labour peer whose son Stephen was killed in 1993, said there were no words that could express what it feels like to have a young person whose "life is still full of possibility, brutally snatched away from you". Writing in the

Guardian, Lady Lawrence said that the hopes and dreams of Cox's family had been "shredded in one foul afternoon".[156]

She also warned that a message of hatred against foreigners or people with different religions had been getting louder in the UK. She singled out for censure the comments made by Johnson about Barack Obama's ancestry and also said that a poster unveiled on the day of Jo Cox's murder by Nigel Farage of UKIP—Boris Johnson's Brexit bedfellow—had been reminiscent of Nazi propaganda.

The poster had presented refugees as a threatening and unwelcome horde overwhelming the country and was captioned: "Breaking Point. We must break free from the EU and take control of our borders."

In a *Guardian* article headed "The mood is ugly, and an MP is dead," the columnist Polly Toynbee accused Boris Johnson and his fellow Brexiters as having "allied themselves to divisive anti-foreigner sentiment ramped up to a level unprecedented in our lifetime".[157]

The Archbishop of York, Dr John Sentamu, had no hesitation in describing Jo Cox as a "martyr, a humanitarian who was slain for her beliefs".[158]

And a few days later, Brendan Cox made a fuller statement to the BBC: "I think she was very worried that the language was coarsening, that people were being driven to take more extreme positions, that people didn't work with each other as individuals and on issues; it was all much too tribal and unthinking. And she was particularly worried—we talked about this regularly—particularly worried about the direction of, not just in the UK but globally, the direction of politics at the moment, particularly around creating division and playing on people's worst fears rather than their best instincts. So we talked about that a lot and it was something that worried her."

When asked by the BBC interviewer, Laura Kuenssberg, whether he thought his wife's death was being used for political ends (Jo Cox had supported the Remain lobby and she wished to stay in Europe), Brendan Cox replied: "She was a politician and she had very strong political views and I believe she was killed because of those views, I think she died because of them." Asked what he would remember about his wife he said: "I will just remember that she met the world with love."[159]

On what would have been her 42nd birthday, thousands watched Jo Cox's widower pay a grief-stricken tribute to her in Trafalgar Square. Brendan Cox's voice choked as he joined his three-year-old daughter and his five-year-old son in a solemn vigil to the murdered MP and he inspired cheers as he repeated his view that "Jo's killing was political. It was an act of terror designed to advance an agenda of hatred towards others. What a beautiful irony it is that an act designed to advance hatred has instead generated such an outpouring of love."

He said that his late wife could "symbolise something much bigger in our country and in our world—something that is under threat," and he added: "She feared the consequences of Europe dividing again." "She hated the idea of building walls between us and worried about the dynamics that could unleash." People were holding up banners reading #LovelikeJo and speakers called it a "show of unity against evil".[160]

There were worldwide vigils in which hundreds attended events in Washington DC, Dublin, Brussels, Oslo, Buenos Aires, Auckland and Beirut. Glastonbury Festival staged a homage from the main stage accompanied by a two-minute silence. Barack Obama paid tribute to the former MP saying that she had transformed the lives of women, children and refugees across the world because of her politics. The US president said he was touched by Cox's "radiant life" and praised her for being an "effective public servant" in her home county of Yorkshire. In an extended post on Facebook, Obama recounted how the MP who died after being shot and stabbed last week had touched his life.

"I did not have the privilege of knowing her," he wrote, "but I know the spirit that defined her life. When I first ran for President, she came to America and volunteered on my campaign.

She gave her time and passion to a country that was not her own because she believed in an idea that transcends borders and cultures—the power of people to bring about change, from the grassroots up."

By contrast, in Boris Johnson's reaction to Jo Cox's killing, Johnson had chosen to tweet a brief message of condolence to the world at large which ended: "Thoughts w/ Jo's family." Brusquely Johnson had abbreviated the word 'with' to a 'w' with a slash, yet he'd not run out of characters for his facile tweet.

Johnson's Brexit mindset would appear to have played a part in fuelling a bullet and a knife. The ugly mood inculcated in the country had empowered Thomas 'Britain First' Mair as he viciously kicked a bleeding mother of two lying wounded on the ground outside the library where she'd just been holding her MP's surgery.

Defenceless and overcome by agonising pain, Jo Cox was forced to endure her assailant, her killer, torturing her and tauntingly hissing out his message of narrow-minded nationalism, "Britain first," as she was dying.

Atavism had been unleashed and as Alex Massie put it in the *Spectator*: "Look. When you encourage rage you cannot then feign surprise when people become enraged. You cannot turn around and say, 'Mate, you weren't supposed to take it so seriously. It's just a game, just a ploy, a strategy for winning votes'."[161]

A headline in the *New York Times* read 'Britain Asks if Tone of Brexit Campaign Made Violence Inevitable'. The American paper went on to quote Alex Massie a little further: "Sometimes rhetoric has consequences," Massie wrote. "If you spend days, weeks, months, years telling people they are under threat, that their country has been stolen from them, that they have been betrayed and sold down the river, that their birth-right has been pilfered, that their problem is they're too slow to realise any of this is happening, that their problem is they're not sufficiently mad as hell, then at some point, in some place, something or someone is going to snap. And then something terrible is going to happen."[162]

© Gerald Scarfe, Sunday Times 19/8/12

10

Undone by the Cuckoo Nest Plot

©Andy Davey 2016

O N 23 JUNE 2016 the long promised referendum resulted in a victory for those who wished to leave the European Union. The impact was immediate. The value of the pound plummeted and share prices fell with a greater velocity than in 2008. Finance companies such as HSBC and Goldman Sachs spoke of moving thousands of jobs from London to Paris. Prime Minister David Cameron announced that he would quit by October and Boris Johnson became the frontrunner to replace him as Conservative leader.

An ominous feeling that the country faced a disastrous meltdown was well expressed by author Matt Carr:

> We now face the possibility of a national and possibly interna-
> tional recession, at a time when the global economy has barely
> recovered from the last one. We are likely to witness the
> breakup and collapse of the United Kingdom; the secession of
> Scotland; the disintegration of the European Union on terms
> set entirely by the far-right.
>
> No one can say for sure how all this will turn out, but it is
> difficult to imagine that the dangerous clowns who led us into
> this mess can negotiate their way through its consequences,
> and there is absolutely nothing to suggest that the final out-
> come will be worth the massive waste of energy and the
> turmoil and uncertainty that it is almost certain to engender.
>
> Already their efforts have divided and polarised the nation,
> after what is perhaps the dirtiest, ugliest and most dishonest
> political campaign in British history. After decades of moving
> away from a society that once had signs up saying 'No blacks or
> Irish', this campaign has unleashed and legitimized toxic
> hatreds, prejudices and expectations that will be difficult, if not
> impossible to put back in the bag.
>
> Brexiters—both left and right—would like to pretend oth-
> erwise—but xenophobia, bigotry, and outright racism have
> been the decisive components of this referendum, which pro-
> duced the dramatic shift towards Leave in the last two
> weeks. The fake promises from Boris Johnson to 'heal' the
> nation—the same Johnson who profited politically from Far-
> age's dogwhistling and engaged in it himself—would be
> laughable if they weren't contemptible.[163]

Those Tories who've been disgusted by the sight of a trium-
phant Johnson and his UKIP side-kick Nigel Farage cracking open
champagne bottles and crowing like cockerels on their respective
dung-hills about 'Independence Day' and about a victory for the
'real, decent people' put together a pressure-group, ABB, which

stands for Anyone But Boris—in their determination to prevent Johnson walking into the top job.

The Conservative Party's Business Minister Anna Soubry spoke of her "anger" at the former mayor of London, who she accused of "confecting his support for Brexit", making a cynical calculation that it would help him to become Prime Minister. She told Channel 4 News: "My anger with Boris is that I don't honestly believe that he believed what he was saying to people, because you look at all the newspaper columns he's ever written, he's never said 'I'm for Out' ... But for his own interests, wanting to be Prime Minister, he went for Leave because it would serve him in his leadership ambitions.

"And I am cross about that because this issue is bigger than any one person. It was about my children, our children's future and our grandchildren's future and now they are seeing the consequences—as we warned and as we said—come to reality."

No doubt Johnson had come to see himself as a cross between Churchill, Lawrence of Arabia, and Odysseus, yet an increasingly unresponsive world was seeing him more and more as a buffoon, as an obstreperous Tigger—a 'twat' is the uncharitable word most frequently used—a persistent blowfly on the body politic that refuses to be swatted away despite his clumsily contaminating all that he touched with his dishonest incompetence.

In a scenario that had all the trappings of a nightmare, it was possible that Johnson's lifelong ambitions would soon be realised, and this nationalist treasure was close to being installed in Downing Street, there perhaps to rally thousands of the unemployed in a job creation scheme involving the rebuilding of Hadrian's Wall, and, for good measure, the building of another wall between Northern and Southern Ireland whilst Britain, the country that he was supposedly governing, began to resemble his sock drawer as he scratched his head in what he hoped would be seen as engaging confusion.

If asked whether Johnson could be trusted as a dog sitter or even to run a bath many people would firmly answer "no", and many more people would regard with some serious apprehension the thought of a clumsy, greedy, violent and meretricious charlatan justifying his government's cuts in honesty as he lumbered round Downing Street clutching the nuclear codes with which to launch a Trident missile.

However, at the eleventh hour this mini-apocalypse was thwarted. The tale now took a dramatic twist. The man who "loves to be loved" was betrayed by one of his closest friends, government justice minister Michael Gove, who announced, "I have come, reluctantly, to the conclusion that Boris cannot provide the leadership or build the team for the task ahead."[164].

Gove had been Johnson's trusted ally in the referendum campaign and he'd known Johnson for almost 30 years since they were contemporaries at the Oxford Union debating society where Gove had backed Johnson's bid to become president of the society in 1986.

In 2005 Gove would recall their undergraduate relationship: "I was Boris's stooge. I became a votary of the Boris cult." Suddenly however Gove announced that rather than continuing to serve as campaign manager in Johnson's bid to become prime minister, he had decided to stand against him as Tory leader.

In Gove's view Johnson "wasn't capable" of the office. Michael Gove, who as a journalist had once called for the return of hanging, was now leaving his friend of half a lifetime to hang out to dry. Despite Johnson's own serial treachery as he climbed the greasy pole of both his career and his concupiscence, it came as a bolt from the blue. He'd only learn of it an hour or two before he was due to announce his candidacy.[165]

Johnson's own paper, the *Daily Telegraph*, reported: "Not since the toppling of Margaret Thatcher 26 years ago has there been a drama on the heroic scale witnessed at Westminster on Thursday. At 9am Mr Johnson was widely assumed to be the favourite to succeed David Cameron as the next Tory leader and prime minister. By midday his career was in tatters."[166]

In an article entitled: "How Boris Johnson was brought to his knees by the 'cuckoo nest plot'", the *Telegraph*'s chief reporter Gordon Rayner wrote: "In Westminster, lobby journalists were reminding each other of Lenin's famous comment that: "There are decades where nothing happens, and there are weeks where decades happen." Except in this case, the time frame was hours, not weeks.

Rayner continued: "Justice Secretary Mr Gove, 48, has for years said he had no ambitions to be prime minister and did not have the skills to be prime minister, making him an ideal deputy for leadership hopeful Boris Johnson—or so Mr Johnson thought."

Tory insiders had been pronouncing the Johnson-Gove combination to be the "dream ticket" but now that Michael Gove had entered the leadership race their man was propelled from favourite to non-runner and Johnson's backers were left gasping.

As one of the most prominent Leave campaigners, Johnson had been widely expected to put himself forward as a potential successor. Instead, on Thursday 30 June 2016, in the front row of a conference room of four-star St Ermin's Hotel in central London, an ashen-faced Johnson stunned his supporters and his enemies alike with the last words of a speech in which he'd recounted his achievements as Mayor of London but then suddenly declared that the next person to lead the Tory party "cannot be me".

He'd been told by his colleagues, including Gove, that he'd be unable to unify the party let alone the country. The *Daily Mail* reported a source as saying that Johnson's team feared Gove would launch a smear campaign against him. "Boris is very unguarded with people close to him and had shared all manner of confidences with Michael during the campaign and there were fears Gove's people are so ruthless it would be dripped out to the media to damage him," said the source.

Johnson could perhaps have anticipated all the skeletons in his cupboard dancing noisily on his coffin and to a jig devised by his former friend. All he could say was 'Et tu, Brute'. Johnson's father, Stanley, chimed in with the same Shakespeare quotation.

Both father and son could see Caesar's laurel crown moving tantalisingly out of reach.

"Boris Johnson peddled lies, half-truths and evasions. Now he's paid the price," was the immediate reaction of Johnson's biographer, Sonia Purnell. In her judgment, "It's not surprising Johnson hasn't entered the race for No 10. But until now he's covered his tracks with bluster and buffoonery" and she recalled something that could certainly have emerged during the white heat of Johnson's race to the top which, if true, was certainly not to Johnson's political credit.

It would seem that Johnson might not have been averse to applying the deviously manipulative skills that he'd learned at Oxford to his being elected to Parliament. Quite unexpectedly Johnson beat a much more highly favoured candidate, one David Platt, in the selection process to become Tory candidate for the safe seat of Henley.

As Sonia Purnell recalled, her biographical researches had revealed that "anonymous letters were distributed, wrongly suggesting Platt was unpatriotically sympathetic to Europe and also gay (when to be so was a career-ender in conservative politics). Platt's girlfriend of the time was dismissed as 'window dressing'. Meanwhile, photographs were quietly circulated of the proudly hetero Johnson with his wife, Marina, in a maternity ward with a newborn baby. The identity of Johnson's mystery helper was never established, nor was any connection to Johnson himself. But the beneficial effect was all too clear."[167]

The implication was that Johnson had been using lies and subterfuge in order to worm his way into Number 10. It would seem, however, that Johnson's manipulative skills were now abandoning him. Relations between Gove and Johnson had deteriorated rapidly in the aftermath of the referendum victory on June 23. Gove had demanded three top jobs in government in exchange for supporting Johnson—that of chancellor, deputy prime minister and chief Brexit negotiator. Johnson's team had advised against accepting Gove's terms on the grounds that it would "put a stranglehold" on Boris' premiership.[168]

The word was that Johnson increasingly feared a backlash from those questioning his integrity, as well he might. Being Brexit's most impassioned tribune, he had left his party in meltdown and the country in chaos, as he thundered his message across the land on every media outlet that "we must take control of our own destiny, take control of our borders" (the latter being code for cutting immigration).

The Governor of the Bank of England announced that since Brexit "the economic outlook had deteriorated" and he compared the mood of the country to post-traumatic stress disorder, laying the blame for the situation on the campaign led by Johnson.

Someone posted the following message on Johnson's Twitter-feed: "Remember the good old days when Bullingdon Club toffs such as David Cameron and Boris Johnson just trashed restaurants not entire economies?"[169]

A far worse consequence was the appalling rise of hate crimes spawned by Brexit in which visitors to the UK and residents alike were assaulted and casually urged to go back where they had come from. The *Daily Mirror* reported: "Racist and xenophobic abuse, attacks and hate crimes are being reported all over the country. And it makes truly harrowing reading." They were evidently being spawned and endorsed by the Brexit result.

The *Mirror* chronicled a plethora of post Brexit racial attacks. Nisha Parti recorded: "I have just been called a p*** by a van driver who refused to stop for me at the zebra crossing. What is going on peeps?"

Dicky Moore recalled for *Channel 4 News*: "My friend just stopped by three men and asked to prove he could speak English. Someone in government get a grip NOW."

James Titcombe tweeted the *Mirror* to tell the paper that his daughter had told him someone at her school had written the name of a Romanian child on the wall in the girls toilets and added "Go back to Romania." Myriam François recorded on

#brexitbacklash: "Walking to mosque last night—two guys shout in my direction 'muzzies out'."

Alice Perry, an Islington Labour Councillor, attested that "Someone came up to one of our black British Cllrs in Sainsbury's and said 'Go back to the jungle you monkey, get out of my f---ing country'."

A number of cards, in both English and Polish, saying "Leave the EU/No more Polish vermin" were found outside St Peter's school in Cambridge by teaching assistants and students, including an eleven-year-old Polish child, who reported they made him feel "really sad".

A Polish cultural centre in Hammersmith was spray-painted with similar messages. An IBRIS Poll showed that some 100,000 Poles in the UK had suffered a "hostile attitude" after the Brexit vote. The *Sunday Times* reported that Ann Korona, who works as a nurse at a GP surgery in London, having come to Britain from Poland in 2008, said she suffered a difficult encounter immediately after the referendum. "I love most of my patients, but the day after the vote one of my elderly patients said to me 'Are you happy that you are going home?' She didn't say it as a joke and I thought it was almost racist. I'm not happy, but I won't go back to Poland".[170]

The wretched Johnson was singled out and blamed for opening these floodgates. In Polly Toynbee's view, "racist graffiti and abuse was given new licence by Boris Johnson, who adopted Nigel Farage's anti-migrant tactics".[171]

The historian Victoria Stiles commented: "I don't think half of the country are racist. I fear that the racists now think half of the country agree with them."[172] The reason being, said author Arun Kundnani that "the Brexit campaign anchored itself on the claim that English life is being destroyed by immigration".

It was a fantasy, with a kernel of truth, said Kundnani. "The post-war social fabric was being destroyed, but the culprits were not Muslim or eastern European immigrants and their alleged enablers in Brussels ... The collapsing United Kingdom now stands as an example of what can befall any society trapped in a free-market economy flailing in its death throes ... Alas, instead of rebelling against the globalization of capital, Britain rebelled against the globalization of labour, finding in the immigrant a suitable object of displaced resentment."[173]

Boris Johnson was suddenly no longer thought to be a national treasure, but rather a white elephant, a political derelict, and with some poetic justice the enormously self-important Johnson found himself marginalised, with the social media largely rejoicing in his demise. The MP for Tottenham, David Lammy tweeted: "Two frivolous Etonians tear the country apart in their own personality feud and get away with it. Then the winner walks away within a week."

Thanks to his lifelong miscalculations, what is Johnson left with? The uncomfortable sensation of a friend's knife grinding into his back. He's been shafted.

"The pisser for Boris," Marina Hyde commented in the *Guardian*, "is that he now can't even contemplate having Michael [Gove] beaten up, like he did that troublesome little journalist back in the day, because many people have one eye on the news at the mo and would probably notice".[174]

Lord Heseltine, elderly Tory grandee and former deputy prime minister, hobbles towards the BBC's cameras to feast upon Johnson's carcass and says he must now "live with the shame of what he's done".

"There will be a profound sense of dismay and frankly contempt. He's ripped the party apart. He's created the greatest constitutional crisis of modern times. He knocked billions off the value of the nation's savings. He's like a general who leads his army to the sound of guns and at the sight of the battlefield abandoned the field. I have never seen so contemptible and irresponsible a situation."

The Tory peer went on to dismiss the contribution of other pro-Leave voices like Mr Gove. "Boris Johnson is the one who won the referendum," he said. "Without him it would not have happened. Without him there would be none of this uncertainty, and he's abandoned the field."[175]

Using more demotic language the *Trainspotting* actor Ewan McGregor tweeted: "You spineless c$&t. You lead this ludicrous campaign to leave EU. Win, and now fuc& off to let someone else clear up your mess."

All that remained was for Johnson's superiority complex and his elitist sense of entitlement to be challenged if not squashed by the British Establishment's moral arbiter, Justin Welby, the Archbishop of Canterbury, who fired this arrow into Johnson's ample frame:

"The events of the last two weeks have led to some of the most dramatic and dynamic changes that we've known," Welby began. "The course of the campaign was unacceptable. Through those comments were created cracks in the thin crust of the politeness and tolerance of our society, through which, since the referendum, we have seen an outwelling of poison and hatred that I cannot remember in this country for very many years."[176]

To other countries what was happening in the UK was mystifying. In the US the comedian John Oliver surmised on his weekly HBO cable show that Brexit had sounded like "a disastrous brand of health bar" and judged its promoter, Boris Johnson, to be "a man with both the look and the economic insights of Bamm Bamm from the Flintstones".

The *Guardian*'s Berlin correspondent Philip Oltermann reported: "A people admired by many Germans as essentially cautious, sceptical, small-c conservatives had flamboyantly gambled with their economic future. Until the feeling sets in that Britain has gambled with Europe's future too, most Germans don't hate the Brits for what happened—they pity them."[177]

The Irish reaction was well expressed in *The Irish Times* by Fintan O'Toole:

We are living with the politics of the fake orgasm. The leaders of the Brexit campaign are obliged to join in with the ecstasies of their followers. They must let out a few polite yelps of satis-

faction. But a week on, it is increasingly clear that theirs is a phony consummation. The earth may have moved—but not for them.

As shown by Boris Johnson's retreat from the prospect of having to actually govern the new kingdom he did so much to create, it was all a performance. It will not be long before those they embraced—the alienated, the dispossessed—realise that they have been had in more ways than one.

The farce of Boris Johnson's abortive leadership bid is just a token of a deeper truth: this is a game of thrones that is all game and no throne.[178]

For Johnson to have changed so much of the outside world's perception of the British character is quite a feat, albeit a negative one. Johnson himself meanwhile is left in a pitiful state through his and his own party's Blackadder-style back-stabbing[179], although few would be inclined to pity him.

Challenged by those critical of his conduct he has seemed however only capable of obscene and impotent expletives. On the day after Johnson pulled out of the race to be Prime Minister, Sonia Purnell wrote:

As mayor, he honed a new technique—the decoy insult. Caught making false claims about the success, or more usually failure, of one of his initiatives or cuts in police staffing, he would regularly light up mayor's question time with a volley of name-calling. His critics were variously Labour stooges, snivelling, illiterate or care in the community. He is standard bearer for a new kind of politics. Last weekend one of his most fervent media supporters told the Today programme—in all apparent seriousness—that 'people want to be lied to'. It is all part of the Johnsonian creed that it is, in his own words, acceptable, sometimes desirable to lie. Certainly that approach has been advantageous to him. But it must come at a price. Johnson paid it yesterday."[180]

It was shown that the promise that had adorned Johnson's Brexit battle bus, namely to give the NHS £350 million a week instead of giving it to the EU, had been spurious if not false. The Brexit victory was a castle built on sand.

As Boris Johnson opened his Islington front door he was greeted with a banner hung from railings opposite that read: BORIS: LIAR, RACIST, OPPORTUNIST.

A passerby holding a mobile phone shouts at him in the street and proffers him the phone insistently, "Here, Boris. I want you to speak to a friend of mine who was the victim of a racist attack yesterday because of you."

A banner featured on the anti-Brexit demonstration in London on 2 July 2016—when at least 30,000 marched from Hyde Park to Parliament Square—was one of many pointing an accusatory finger at Boris Johnson. Cuttingly it read: "You stole our future from us".

Johnson's hardcore supporters determine that he will rise again from the ashes and Johnson himself, rather than take his defeat lying down, has been left desperate for a forum for his opinions, and for any kind of media attention, almost as if it were an addiction. But, for the time being at least, 10 Downing Street has been spared from imminent shark attack.

However it is notable that this "sociopathic monstrosity," in Matt Carr's phrase[181], was energetically built up over several years and enthusiastically promoted by the Conservative party as a cult figure, to the point where he was a short step from being British prime minister. This surely speaks volumes.

11

The Man With No Moral Compass

©Steve Bell 2016

THERESA MAY, arriving at Downing Street on 13 July 2016 to take up her new role as prime minister, vowed to lead a government that worked for all, and not just for the "privileged few", as she put it. To this end, and on the same day, she appointed one of the most privileged few in the country to serve as her Foreign Secretary.

The undiplomatic Boris Johnson is to be Britain's leading diplomat. Will he be able to restrain himself from trying out his prize-winning *Spectator* limerick about the Turkish Head of State on President Erdogan in which: "A young fellow from Ankara/ Who was a terrific wankerer / Until he sowed his wild oats/ With the help of a goat"? The world awaits the re-release of Boris's bestial squib with bated breath for no gaffe is now off-limits.

The most indiscreet man in public life will now also be in charge of MI6 and GCHQ: a man with no moral compass is in charge of a senior department of military intelligence and a lying journalist becomes the Chief Panjandrum of the doughnut-shaped surveillance centre.

On learning this farcical news the *Daily Mirror* suggested that "Britain's credibility will now be hanging by a thread" and it illustrated its front-page story with a photograph of the ludicrous Johnson stranded in mid-air on a zip-wire in a publicity stunt that went wrong.[182]

The *Mirror* was right and the world reacted with bewildered horror, disbelief and ridicule. When the US State Department spokesman Mark Toner heard the news, he struggled to keep a straight face and the American political scientist, Ian Bremmer, hoped that it might all be a joke. "Maybe the Brits are just having us on. We probably deserve it."

The Berlin correspondent of German public broadcaster ZDF, Nicole Diekmann, tweeted: "So, Boris Johnson, foreign minister. British humour." ZDF's Brussels correspondent, Anne Gellinek, said that Johnson was "properly, properly hated" and was seen as "the head of a campaign of lies" in the EU's headquarters. Simone Peter, co-leader of the German Green Party, likened Johnson's appointment to "trusting the cat to keep the cream". [183]

The French Foreign Minister, Jean-Marc Ayrault, said despondently: "During the campaign he lied a lot to the British people. I need a partner with whom I can negotiate and who is clear, credible and reliable." His appalled reaction was echoed by Johnson's audience when, shortly after his appointment, Johnson appeared at the French Embassy only to be soundly booed and jeered.[184]

Germany's foreign minister, Frank-Walter Steinmeier, condemned Johnson's conduct in the run-up to the EU referendum as "deceitful and reckless" and he called the new foreign secretary's behaviour *ungeheuerlich*, meaning outrageous. "People in the UK are experiencing a rude awakening after irresponsible politicians first lured the country into Brexit and then, once the decision was made, decided to bolt from responsibility, and instead go off and play cricket."

Frans Timmermans, the European Commission's vice president, said that Johnson's comments had been spreading "hatred" in a way he wouldn't have believed possible in Britain.

Meanwhile, Boris Johnson's neighbours, feeling the need to apologise on his behalf, fixed a notice to the railings of his house which read in capital letters: SORRY WORLD.

By contrast, at his first Foreign Office press conference—held jointly with U.S. Secretary of State John Kerry—Boris Johnson gave his latest reworking of "sorry, but not sorry". When challenged about his insults to men, women, races, cities, countries and continents, Johnson arrogantly declared: "It would really take me too long to engage in a fully global itinerary of apology to all concerned."[185]

Theresa May once spoke of her regret that the Tory Party was known as "the nasty party". Her ill-starred appointment ensured that its malign character would be maintained for some time to come. And it may have taken Boris Johnson one slavering step closer to realizing his lifelong dream of becoming Prime Minister.

©Gerald Scarfe, Sunday Times, 10/5/14

Notes

[1] Waitrose is an upmarket British supermarket chain.

[2] BNP is the abbreviation for the far-right British National Party.

[3] Isabel Oakeshott, "Gadzooks, Boris admits bumbling is a cunning plan," *Sunday Times* (14 April 2013).

[4] Harry Mount, "Here comes Boris" *Spectator* (9 August 2014).

[5] Simon Heffer, "The Guest Column," *New Statesman* (4–10 March 2016).

[6] Estelle Shirbon, "Boris for prime minister? *Reuters* (5 May 2015). http://uk.reuters.com/article/uk-britain-election-boris-idUKKBN0NQ0U620150505

[7] *Observer* (5 October 2003).

[8] *Daily Telegraph* (16 February 1996).

[9] *Spectator* (2 February 2002).

[10] *Spectator* (2 February 2002).

[11] Bob Roberts, "Boris Johnson race row fury," *Mirror* (2 February 2012). http://www.mirror.co.uk/news/uk-news/boris-johnson-race-row-fury-527310

[12] Patrick Wintour, political editor: *Guardian* (4 August 2007).

[13] *Spectator* (16 November 2002).

[14] *Spectator* (11 January 2003).

[15] *Spectator* (24 February 2001). Sonia Purnell, *Just Boris: a tale of blond ambition*, (London: Aurum Press, 2012), 193.

[16] Lester Holloway, *Media Diversified* (16 April 2016). https://mediadiversified.org/2016/04/16/forget-politics-for-the-spectator-when-it-comes-to-race-addressing-inequality-is-going-too-far/

[17] Ibid.

[18] Nigel Cawthorne, *Blond Ambition: The Rise and Rise of Boris Johnson* (Endeavour Press, 2015), 50.

[19] Ibid., 55.

[20] Purnell, *Just Boris*, 342.

[21] Boris Johnson, *Friends, voters, countrymen* (HarperCollins, 2001), 96.

[22] Denis MacShane, *Brexit: How Britain Will Leave Europe* (I.B.Tauris, 2015), 207.

[23] Dennis Rahkonen, "Each Day, Capitalism Kills far more Innocents Than Died on 9/11," *Dissident Voice* (3 April 2009).

[24] Ronald Reagan, 1981.

[25] Richard Hebditch, "Pedestrians and pedallers unite!" *Guardian* (12 March 2008).

[26] Darren Johnson, "Are London's roads really getting safer?" *Left Foot Forward* (15 June 2015).

[27] Purnell, *Just Boris*, 171.

[28] Ibid., 172. Boris Johnson, *Life in the Fast Lane* (London: Harper Perennial, 2007), 239.

[29] *Daily Telegraph* (26 February 2004).

[30] Boris Johnson, *Lend Me Your Ears* (Harper Collins, 2004), 317.

[31] Boris Johnson, *Have I Got Views for You* (Harper Collins, 2008), 272.

[32] Leader entitled "Infantile resentment" in *Spectator* (22 November 2003), 7.

[33] Boris Johnson, *Lend me your ears*, 464.

[34] Boris Johnson, "The holy impulse that can lead to dinner with a despot," *Daily Telegraph* (9 Aug 2010).

[35] Andrew Gimson, *Boris: The Rise of Boris Johnson*, (Simon & Schuster, 2012), 98.

[36] Gimson, *Boris*, 93.

[37] Simon Hoggart, "Boris Johnson has been brought to his knees by a man who died in 1312," *Guardian* (25 March, 2013).

[38] Peter Walker, "Boris Johnson: Eddie Mair did 'a splendid job'," *Guardian* (25 March 2013).

[39] Cawthorne, *Blond Ambition*, 29.

[40] Gimson, *Boris*, 57.

[41] MacShane, *Brexit*, 174.

[42] John Palmer, "Thatcher sets face against united Europe", *The Guardian* (21 September 1988)

[43] Ibid., 172–173.

[44] Boris Johnson, *The Annual Margaret Thatcher Lecture* (27 November 2013).

[45] Caroline Wheeler, EU seeks control of our coasts, *Daily Express* (7 March 2016)

[46] Boris Johnson, "There's a simple solution to this Euro-elections sham," *Daily Telegraph* (27 April 2014).

[47] Purnell, *Just Boris*, 201.

[48] Ibid., 43.

[49] Ibid., 395.

[50] Ibid., 386-387.

[51] According to Nigel Cawthorne, this has now risen to £500,00 p.a.

[52] Purnell, *Just Boris*, 73.

[53] Ibid., 72.

[54] Ibid., 73.

[55] Ibid., 340, 341.

[56] Ibid.

[57] Gimson, *Boris*, 68-69.

[58] Ibid., 74-75.

[59] Purnell, *Just Boris*, 69.

[60] Gimson, *Boris*, 259.

[61] Simon Walters, "Boris, Petsy and a 'pyramid of piffle," *Mail on Sunday* (7 November 2004)

[62] Purnell, *Just Boris*, 261.

[63] Gimson, *Boris*, 407.

[64] Max Hastings, *Daily Mail* (9 October 2012).

[65] Michael Wolff, "The Boris Show," *Vanity Fair* (29 April 2008).

[66] Boris Johnson, "Killing deer to save them," *Daily Telegraph* (9 July 1997). Re-published in Johnson, *Lend Me Your Ears*. Gimson, *Boris*, 26.

[67] Boris Johnson, "If we want to be taken seriously, we have to defend ourselves," *Telegraph* (16 February 2016).

[68] Adam Withnail, "Royal Navy investigates Trident whistle-blower William McNeilly who claims nuclear programme is a 'disaster waiting to happen," *Independent on Sunday* (17 May 2015).

[69] ABJ stands for Alexander Boris Johnson. An Oppidan (lit. town-dweller) is the name of fee-paying Eton students who live in boarding houses in the town of Eton. The Wall Game is played between Oppidans and Scholars who wear gowns and are known as 'Tugs', being short for togati or gown-wearers. (Johnson was a 'tug'.)

[70] Gimson, *Boris*, 55.

[71] Barney Ronay, "Young, rich and drunk," *Guardian* (9 May 2008).

[72] Ronay, "Young, rich and drunk."

[73] Evelyn Waugh, *Brideshead Revisited* (London: Chapman and Hall, 1945; Penguin Books, 2001), 43.

[74] Waugh, *Decline and Fall* (London: Chapman and Hall, 1928), 7.

[75] Joy Lo Dico, "The Sikorski set", *Evening Standard* (26 June 2014).

[76] Ronay, "Young, rich and drunk."

[77] Tom McTague, "Bullingdon Club initiation ceremony," *Daily Mirror* (23 February 2013).

[78] Andrew Sparrow, *Guardian* (4 October 2009); Purnell, *Just Boris*, 406.

[79] Boris Johnson, "In Defence of Public Schools," *The Eton Chronicle* (12 December 1980).

[80] *Evening Standard* (19 January 2010). Cited by Purnell, *Just Boris*, 201.

[81] *When Boris Met Dave*, Channel 4, October 2009.

[82] I am indebted to Martin Soames for this reaction to the Bullingdon Club photograph in a private communication.

[83] Gimson, *Boris*, 117.

[84] Darius Guppy, *Roll the Dice: A True Saga of Love, Money and Betrayal* (Blake Publishing, 1996), 102.

[85] Audio available on Soundcloud and transcript here: http://boris-johnson.blogspot.co.uk/search/label/darius%20guppy

[86] Marcus Scriven, "Words of Dishonour: Boris Johnson and 'Guppygate'," What's Next Journal (First published in the *Mail on Sunday* 16 July 1995). http://www.whatnextjournal.org.uk/

[87] Richard Pendlebury, "The high society psycho who has come back to haunt Boris Johnson," *Daily Mail* (4 April 2009).

[88] Transmitted 24 March 2013 on BBC2.

[89] Darius Guppy, "Admits to horrifying attack on journalist 'who insulted his wife'," *Daily Mail* (12 July 2013).

[90] Ibid.

[91] Peter Stanford, "Darius Guppy: 'That element of madness was always there'," *Telegraph* (29 March 2013). *Daily Mail* (12 July 2013).

[92] Darius Guppy, "Who will bully the bullies?" *New Statesman* (11 July 2013).

[93] Andy McSmith, "Darius, Boris and a blast from the past," *Independent* (30 March 2009).

[94] Guppy, *Roll the Dice*, 3.

[95] c.f. Purnell, *Just Boris*.

[96] Andy Newman, "Boris Johnson on Law and Order," *Socialist Unity* (2 April 2008). http://socialistunity.com

[97] Purnell, *Just Boris,* 128.

[98] Gimson, *Boris*, 108.

[99] Ibid., 104.

[100] *Daily Telegraph* (15 September 2003).

[101] MacShane, *Brexit*, 175.

[102] Gimson, *Boris*, 99.

[103] Purnell, *Just Boris*, 115.

[104] BBC (20 October 2005).

[105] Purnell, *Just Boris*, 128.

[106] Leader, "Bigley's fate. We have lost our sense of proportion about what constitutes a tragedy." *Spectator* (16 October 2004).

[107] Purnell, *Just Boris*, 254-255.

[108] Thomas Jones, "Boris Johnson: The Blond Beast of Brexit; A Study in Depravity," *Organized Rage* (31 May 2016). http://www.organizedrage.com

[109] Robert F. Lynch, Robert L. Trivers, "Self-deception inhibits laughter," *Elsevier* 53, no. 4, (September 2012): 491–495.

[110] Christopher Bollas, *Being a Character: Psychoanaysis and Self-Experience*, (London: Routledge, 1993).

[111] Purnell, *Just Boris*, 88.

[112] Gimson, *Boris*, 101.

[113] Her remark was made to Sir Eric Anderson, Johnson's former Headmaster. Gimson, *Boris*, 104.

[114] Darius Guppy, "My old friend Boris is wrong on Brexit," *New Statesman* (4–10 March 2016).

[115] *Daily Telegraph* (15 September 2003); see also Purnell, *Just Boris*, 120.

[116] Rowena Mason, "David Cameron boasts of 'brilliant' UK arms exports to Saudi Arabia," *Guardian* (25 February 2016).

[117] Jeremy Corbyn, "Cameron's deal is the wrong one: but Britain must stay in Europe," *Guardian* (20 February 2016).

[118] Arif Durrani, "Boris Johnson welcomes 'benevolent' Murdoch and News UK to London Bridge," *Media Week* (17 September 2014).

[119] Richard Neville, "The Life and Crimes of a Global Goebbels," *Counterpunch* (1 September 2006).

[120] Anthony Hilton, "Stay or go the lack of solid facts means it's all a leap of faith," *Evening Standard* (25 February 2016).

[121] Michael Wolff, "The Boris Show," *Vanity Fair* (29 April 2008).

[122] *The Spectator* (21 September 2015).

[123] Michael Crick, "The story behind David Cameron and Boris Johnson's battle over Europe," *Radio Times*, (25 May 2016).

[124] James Kirkup, "A wrestling match between Boris Johnson and David Cameron reveals the true nature of their rivalry," *Daily Telegraph* (21 Feb 2016).

[125] James Kirkup, "Boris Johnson: I'd love to replace 'Cameron Minor' as PM," *Daily Telegraph* (19 March 2013).

[126] Tim Shipman, "Palace fights to save Queen's independence: Brexit row has damaged her, admit courtiers," *Sunday Times* (13 March 2016).

[126] "A Peculiar Messiah," *Economist* (25 April 2015).

[127] Tom Newton Dunn and Harry Cole, "Who let the hogs out?" *Sun* (21 September 2015).

[128] Jon Stone, "The cost of replacing Trident is really £167bn, new figures suggest," *Independent* (25 October 2015).

[129] "A Peculiar Messiah," *Economist* (25 April 2015).

[130] Boris Johnson, *The Dream of Rome, with new material on the rise of Islam* (Harper Perennial, 2007), 188.

[131] Nick Cohen, "Boris Johnson: Everything about you is phoney," *Spectator* (22 February 2016).

[132] Jerry Hayes, "Boris is a copper bottomed, double dealing hypocritical little shit. The press will destroy him," http://jerryhayes.co.uk

[133] "As Boris was growing up whenever anyone asked him what he wanted to be, he would answer: 'World King'," Rachel Johnson, interviewed in "Boris Johnson: The Irresistible Rise," Transmitted 24 March, 2013 on BBC2.

[134] *Evening Standard* (9 April 2010).

[135] Anushka Asthana and Ben Quinn, "London mayor under fire for remark about 'part-Kenyan' Barack Obama," *Guardian* (22 April 2016).

[136] "Obama hits back at Boris Johnson's alleged smears," *BBC News* (22 April 2016).

[137] Cawthorne, *Blond Ambition*, 114.

[138] Ibid., 118.

[139] Adam Vaughan and Esther Addley, "Boris Johnson held back negative findings of air pollution report," *Guardian* (17 May 2016).

[140] Pippa Crerar and Joe Murphy, "Boris: Water cannon ban shows Government is trying to clip my wings," *Evening Standard* (16 July 2015).

[141] Gareth Furby, "Unused Met Police water cannon location revealed," *BBCNews* (15 February 2016).

[142] Damien Gayle, "Water cannon bought by Boris Johnson to be sold off without being used," Guardian (1 July 2016).

[143] Purnell, *Just Boris*, 7.

[144] Rachel Dale, "The Mayor of London's late-night tirade caught on camera," *Sun* (17 June 2015).

[145] Purnell, *Just Boris*, 7.

[146] Jack Hill, "You are in the place where James Bond shoots the evil baddie," *Times* (27 February 2016).

[147] "'Proud Londoner' Damian Lewis slams Boris Johnson over 'Dubai on Thames' promise," *Daily Mail* (5 May 2016).

[148] Rowan Moore, "Boris Johnson's dire legacy for London," *Observer* (10 April 2016).

[149] Matthew Parris, "Tories have got to end their affair with Boris," *Times* (26 March 2016).

[150] Nick Cohen, "Boris Johnson. Liar, conman – and prime minister?" *Guardian* (26 March 2016).

[151] James Forsyth and Fraser Nelson, "Boris needs you! The former mayor of London makes his case for Brexit," *Spectator* (14 May 2016).

[152] Michael Deacon, "Amber Rudd v Boris Johnson: live on ITV, the Tory party just tore itself apart," *Daily Telegraph* (9 June 2016).

[153] Yves Smith, "British MP Jo Cox Murdered in Presumed Brexit-Related Attack," *Naked Capitalism* (16 June 2016). http://www.nakedcapitalism.com

[154] "Jo Cox MP death. Thomas Mair in Court on Murder Charge," *BBCNews* (18 June 2016).

[155] Patrick Wintour, "Mainstream politicians 'clueless on migration debate', says Jo Cox's husband," *Guardian* (17 June 2016).

[156] Robert Booth, Vikram Dodd, Kevin Rawlinson and Nicola Slawson, "Jo Cox murder suspect tells court his name is 'death to traitors, freedom for Britain' *Guardian* (18 June 2016).

[157] Polly Toynbee, "The mood is ugly, and an MP is dead. It's wrong to view the killing of Jo Cox in isolation. Hate has been whipped up against the political class," *Guardian* (16 June 2016).

[158] Neil Berry, "Brexit's first victim," *Arab News* (20 June 2016).

[159] Rowena Mason, "Jo Cox's husband says she was killed because of her political views", Guardian (21 June 2016)

[160] Mikey Smith and Dan Bloom, "Jo Cox vigil: Husband Brendan leads emotional Trafalgar Square vigil to mark murdered MP's birthday," *Daily Mirror* (22 June 2016).

[161] Alan Massie, "A Day of Infamy," *Spectator* (16 June 2016).

[162] Steven Erlanger, "Britain Asks if Tone of 'Brexit' Campaign Made Violence Inevitable," *New York Times* (17 June 2016).

[163] Matt Carr, "Freaky Friday," *Matt Carr's Infernal Machine*, http://infernalmachine.co.uk/freaky-friday (25 June 2016).

[164] Gordon Rayner, "How Boris Johnson was brought to his knees by the 'cuckoo nest plot'" *Daily Telegraph* (1 July 2016).

[165] Rowena Mason and Heather Stewart, "Gove's thunderbolt and Boris's breaking point: a shocking Tory morning," *Guardian* (30 June 2016).

[166] Philip Johnston, "Like Michael Heseltine, Boris Johnson was in prime position – but knife wielders never wear the crown," *Daily Telegraph* (30 June 2016).

[167] Sonial Purnell, *Guardian* (1 July 2016).

[168] Simon Walters, "'I was a fool to trust Gove': Boris Johnson told aides he feared a smear campaign unless he quit race after his Brexit betrayer demanded THREE top jobs in Government," *Daily Mail* (2 July 2016).

[169] Teacher Dude @teacherdude tweeted #BorisJohnson https://twitter.com/teacherdude

[170] Dipesh Gadher, Tom Harper, and Jakub Krupa, "Remainers shake family trees in bid to pick up EU passports," *Sunday Times* (3 July 2016).

[171] Polly Toynbee, "This is now Project Betrayal – and we are all the victims: the Brexiters were led by fantasists. As recession threatens, did the voters take back control? No," *Guardian* (27 June 2016).

[172] Victoria Stiles @ViolettaCrisis https://twitter.com/ViolettaCrisis

[173] Arun Kundnani, "The Right-Wing Populism That Drove Brexit Can Only Be Fought With A Genuinely Radical Alternative", http://www.alternet.org/world/right-wing-populism-drove-brexit-can-only-be-fought-genuinely-radical-alternative, (2 July 2016)

[174] Marina Hyde, "Bye bye, Boris, the man who wouldn't clear up his own mess," *Guardian* (30 June 2016).

[175] Josh May, Lord Heseltine "Boris Johnson must 'live with the shame' of his actions," https://www.politicshome.com/ (30 June 2016).

[176] https://www.politicshome.com/news/europe/eu-policy-agenda/brexit/news/76966/archbishop-canterbury-eu-referendum-has-created

[177] Philip Olterman, "What do Germans think about Brexit? They pity us," *Guardian* (28 June 2016).

[178] Fintan O'Toole, 'Brexit and the politics of the fake orgasm' *The Irish Times*, (July2, 2016)

[179] The plots of *Blackadder*, one of the most popular British sitcoms ever, centred on endless betrayals and backstabbings.

[180] Sonia Purnell, "Johnson peddled lies, half-truths and evasions. Now he's paid the price," *Guardian* (1 July 2016).

[181] Matt Carr, "Labour Plotters: Stop your Sobbing" http://infernalmachine.co.uk/labour-plotters-stop-your-sobbing (30 June 2016)

[182] "Britain faces being a laughing stock after Boris Johnson is made Foreign Secretary by Theresa May", *Daily Mirror*, (14 July 2016).

[183] "'Maybe the Brits are just having us on': the world reacts to Boris Johnson as foreign minister", *Guardian*, (14 July 2016).

[184] "Boris Johnson 'booed' during his first speech as Foreign Secretary", *Daily Telegraph*, (14 July 2016).

[185] Simon Lewis, "Boris Johnson Says It Would Take Too Long to Apologize for 'Thesaurus' of Insults", *Time,* (20 July 20 2016)

Acknowledgements

Robin Beste, Andrew Burgin, Carrie Giunta, Lesley Brooks, Tom Crewe, Daniel Soar, Kate Hudson, Martin Wilkinson, Richard Adams, Jonangus Mackay, Clem Shaw, Dennis Harrison, Eddie Mizzi, Jan Woolf, Clare Brant, Nigel Allen, Graham Yates, Markus Karsten, Rudiger Gruenhagen, Lutz Kroth, Thomas Jones, Mary-Kay Wilmers, Simon Drake, Natalia de la Ossa, Niall McDevitt, China Williams, Roy Hutchins, Elena Caldera, Lily Williams, Ben Hall, Shaun Whiteside, Dave Motion and Claire Palmer

EARLIER DRAFT

This book updates and expands substantially an earlier draft of the text published in May 2016 prior to the EU referendum by the *London Review of Books* under the title: *Boris Johnson: the Beast of Brexit. A Study in Depravity.*

The Cartoonists

Many thanks to Steve Bell, Peter Brookes, Dave Brown, Andy Davey, Martin Rowson, Gerald Scarfe and Ralph Steadman, who contributed their cartoons to this book.

©*Martin Rowson 2016: Ultimate Nightmare - Donald Trump and Boris Johnson*